Library of
Davidson College

HOLY MOTHERS
Werner Schwab

PARROTS' LIES
Andreas Marber

JAMAICA
Oliver Bukowski

MALARIA
Simone Schneider

Other Volumes in the International Collection

AUSTRALIA PLAYS
ed. Katharine Parsons
Jack Davis: *No Sugar*
Alma de Groen: *The Rivers of China*
Michael Gow: *Away*
Louis Nowra: *The Golden Age*
David Williamson: *Travelling North*
ISBN 1 85459 056 1

THE CRACK IN THE EMERALD
New Irish Plays ed. David Grant
Dermot Bolger:
　The Lament for Arthur Cleary
Marina Carr: *Low in the Dark*
Michael Harding: *The Misogynist*
Marie Jones: *The Hamster Wheel*
ISBN 1 85459 237 8

CZECH PLAYS
ed. Barbara Day
Vaclav Havel: *Tomorrow!*
Ivan Klima: *Games*
Josef Topol: *Cat on the Rails*
Daniela Fischerova: *Dog and Wolf*
ISBN 1 85459 074 X

DUTCH PLAYS
ed. Della Couling
Lodewijk de Boer:
　The Buddha of Ceylon
Judith Herzberg: *The Wedding Party*
Arne Sierens: *Drummers*
Karst Woudstra: *Burying the Dog*
Frans Strijards:
　The Stendhal Syndrome
ISBN 1 85459 289 0

GERMAN PLAYS
ed. Elyse Dodgson
Anna Langhoff: *The Table Laid*
Dea Loher: *Stranger's House*
Klaus Pohl: *Waiting Room Germany*
D. Rust: *Jennifer Klemm*
ISBN 1 85459 338 2

HUNGARIAN PLAYS
ed. László Upor
András Nagy. *The Seducer's Diary*
Andor Szilágyi: *Unsent Letters*
Ákos Németh: *Muller's Dances*
Péter Kárpáti: *Everywoman*
ISBN 1 85459 244 0

LATIN AMERICAN PLAYS
ed. Sebastian Doggart
Octavio Paz: *Rapaccini's Daughter*
Jose Triana:
　Night of the Assassins
Griselda Gambaro: *Saying Yes*
Carlos Fuentes:
　Orchids in the Moonlight
Mario Vargas Llosa:
　Mistress of Desires
ISNB 1 85459 249 1

SOUTH AFRICAN PLAYS
ed. Stephen Gray
Anthony Akerman:
　Somewhere on the Border
Maishe Maponya:
　The Hungry Earth
Susan Pam-Grant:
　Curl Up and Dye
Paul Slabolepszy: *Over the Hill*
Pieter-Dirk Uys: *Just Like Home*
ISBN 1 85459 148 7

SPANISH PLAYS
ed. Elyse Dodgson & Mary Peate
Sergi Belbel: *Caresses*
Juan Mayorga: *The Scorched
　Garden*
David Planell: *Bazaar*
Antonio Onetti: *Bleeding Heart*
Lluïsa Cunillé: *Roundabout*
Paloma Pedrero: *Wolf Kisses*
ISBN 1 85459 418 4

GERMAN PLAYS 2

Selected and edited by Elyse Dodgson
and David Tushingham

WERNER SCHWAB ■ HOLY MOTHERS
Translated by Meredith Oakes

ANDREAS MARBER ■ PARROTS' LIES
Translated by David Tushingham

OLIVER BUKOWSKI ■ JAMAICA
Translated by David Spencer

SIMONE SCHNEIDER ■ MALARIA
Translated by Penny Black

Introduction by David Tushingham

THE INTERNATIONAL COLLECTION

NICK HERN BOOKS
London
in association with the Goethe-Institut
and the Royal Court Theatre

A Nick Hern Book

German Plays 2 first published in Great Britain in 1999 as an original paperback by Nick Hern Books Limited, 14 Larden Road, London W3 7ST

Die Präsidentinnen (Holy Mothers) copyright © Werner Schwab 1999
Translation copyright © Meredith Oakes 1999
Published in this edition by special permission of Oberon Books

Die Lügen der Papagaien (Parrots' Lies) copyright © Andreas Marber 1999
Translation copyright © David Tushingham 1999

'Til Denver (Jamaica) copyright © Oliver Bukowski 1999
Translation copyright © David Spencer 1999

Malaria (Malaria) copyright © Simone Schneider 1999
Translation copyright © Penny Black 1999

Foreword copyright © Elyse Dodgson 1999
Introduction copyright © David Tushingham 1999

The authors of the original plays and the translators have asserted their moral rights

Typeset by Country Setting, Kingsdown, Kent CT14 8ES
Printed and bound in Great Britain by Athenaeum Press Ltd, Gateshead

A CIP catalogue record for this book is available from the British Library

ISBN 1 85459 479 6

CAUTION All rights whatsoever in these plays and translations are strictly reserved. Requests to reproduce the text in whole or in part should be addressed to the publisher. Applications for performance anywhere in the world of any of these plays in the translations printed here whether in excerpt or in full should be made as follows:-

Holy Mothers **Amateurs and Professionals**: Mel Kenyon, Casarotto Ramsay and Associates Ltd, 60-66 Wardour Street, London W1V 4ND *fax* +44(0)207 287 9128

Parrots' Lies **Amateurs and Professionals:** Nick Hern Books, 14 Larden Road, London W3 7ST *fax* +44(0)208 746 2006 *e-mail*: info@nickhernbooks.demon.co.uk in co-operation with Hartmann & Stauffacher, D-50672 Köln, Bismarckstrasse 36, Germany.

Jamaica **Amateurs:** Nick Hern Books (as above). **Professionals:** Leah Schmidt, The Agency, 24 Pottery Lane, London W11 4LZ *fax* +44(0)207 727 9037. **Both:** in co-operation with Gustav Kiepenheuer Bühnenvertriebs-Gmbh, Schweinfurthstrasse 60, D-14195 Berlin (Dahlem), Germany.

Malaria **Amateurs:** Nick Hern Books (as above). **Professionals:** Alan Brodie Representation, 211 Piccadilly, London W1V 9LD *fax* +44(0)207 917 2872. **Both:** in co-operation with Gustav Kiepenheuer (as above).

No performance may take place unless a licence has been obtained. Application must be made before rehearsals begin. Performance includes recitation, lecturing, public reading, broadcasting and television.

Contents

Preface
by Barbara Honrath vii

Foreword
by Elyse Dodgson ix

Introduction
by David Tushingham xi

HOLY MOTHERS
by Werner Schwab
translated by Meredith Oakes 1

PARROTS' LIES
by Andreas Marber
translated by David Tushingham 39

JAMAICA
by Oliver Bukowski
translated by David Spencer 99

MALARIA
by Simone Schneider
translated by Penny Black 157

Acknowledgements

We would like to thank the following for all their commitment to this project:

The writers, translators, readers, directors and actors who took part in the 1997 *New German Voices* Season at the Royal Court, the British Council who supported the work of the exchange in Germany, Andreas Beck, Elisabeth Fibich, Natalie Highwood, Jens Hilljé, Aurélie Merél, Sylviana Ollennu, Thomas Ostermeier, Mary Peate, Ian Rickson, Friedrich Schirmer and Graham Whybrow

Preface

In December 1997 the Royal Court Theatre hosted a German Playreading Season, its third since 1993, organised in association with the Goethe-Institut London. The season featured five plays by new playwrights from German-speaking countries in specially commissioned English translations. We are delighted that four of these plays which had not been published previously are now made accessible in print.

The plays in this volume deal with a wide variety of themes which are of concern to contemporary German society. Although the main focus is on comedy, these plays reveal, in a dazzling variety of tones, different styles of new German drama. As a result, they offer a very vivid and complex picture of current sociopolitical and cultural issues as well as theatrical trends in Germany.

Both the readings of new German plays at the Royal Court and their publication are part of an ongoing exchange between playwrights and theatre practitioners from Britain and Germany which also involves the presentation, every two years, of new British plays in Berlin. This project, supported by the British Council, was initiated by the Royal Court in conjunction with the Deutsches Theater and was developed with the young artistic team at its studio theatre, the Baracke. This team has now taken charge of the Schaubühne which will also be the new German venue for the British-German dialogue.

In London, the huge success of the rehearsed readings of new German plays is due above all to the enormous commitment and enthusiasm of Elyse Dodgson and her colleagues at the International Department of the Royal Court Theatre. No other theatre in Britain has such a long tradition of encouraging and supporting new writing for the stage. The Royal Court is therefore an ideal forum for the introduction of contemporary

German plays to a British audience. As well as working with outstanding actors and directors, the Royal Court is adept in creating a stimulating atmosphere for debate between the German playwrights and authors, directors, critics, and other theatre experts from the UK. Last but not least, Elyse Dodgson always selects excellent translators, and the high quality of their translations is clearly a key factor in the plays' success.

Of the four plays in this collection, one will have had a fully fledged production in London at the time of publication. We hope that this volume may inspire many more theatre directors in English-speaking countries to present further productions of these plays.

Barbara Honrath
Head of Arts
Goethe-Institut London

Foreword

The Royal Court Theatre set up an exchange with new playwrights from Germany in 1992. Since then eleven German writers and directors have attended the four week Royal Court International Residency. The relationship with our partners, the Deutsches Theater Baracke, Berlin began in 1994. We have exchanged hundreds of plays and over 30 British and German playwrights have travelled to Berlin and London to take part in the exchange. In 1999 the exchange moved with the artistic team of Thomas Ostermeier and Jens Hilljé to the world famous Schaubühne Theater, Berlin.

The plays in this volume were selected for rehearsed readings for the New German Voices Week in December 1997. This was presented as part of the Royal Court International Writers' Festival in the Theatre Upstairs. The most recent week of readings of new German plays supported by the Goethe Institut took place in November 1999 and included the playwrights David Gieselmann, Katerina Gericke, Teresia Walser, Mortiz Rinke and Marius Von Mayenburg. Gieselmann and Von Mayenburg are now part of the Schaubühne team and both took part in the Royal Court International Residency in 1998 and 1999.

In May 1999 the Royal Court co-produced Werner Schwab's *Die Präsidentinnen (Holy Mothers)* at the New Ambassadors Theatre in the translation we commissioned by Meredith Oakes. David Gieselmann's *Herr Kolpert (Mr Kolpert)* and Marius Von Mayenburg's *Feuergesicht (Fireface)* will have full productions in the Royal Court in May 2000. The Baracke in turn has produced successful productions of previous exchange plays: Mark Ravenhill's *Shopping and Fucking*, Jim Cartwright's *I licked a Slag's Deodorant* and Sarah Kane's *Blasted.* In September 1998 the Baracke hosted writers Rebecca Prichard, Tim Luscombe and Ed Thomas.

In January 2000 I visited Berlin with Literary Manager Graham Whybrow for the opening of the Schaubühne. The first season included the German language premiere of Sarah Kane's *Crave*. While the new theatre is inviting submissions of new German plays, the Gorky Theatre is staging twenty short plays by new authors down the road in a special season at the Schiller Theatre. These are just two examples of the appetite for new writing in theatres all over Germany. We can see that our exchange has developed into a thriving association of ideas, working methods and most of all plays and playwrights. The plays in this volume demonstrate why new writing is becoming important again in German theatre.

Elyse Dodgson
Associate Director
Head of International Department
Royal Court Theatre
February 2000

Introduction

I'm looking through the programme for a production of Werner Schwab's *Die Präsidentinnen* (translated here by Meredith Oakes as *Holy Mothers*), staged by Austria's leading theatre, the Vienna Burgtheater.

What I find striking about it is not so much my personal memories of the show, which was superb, or the bizarre circumstances under which I saw it, a festival in Pilsen which involved a number of dignitaries in suits giving speeches from a stage designed to resemble a giant arse complete with larger-than-life pubic hair. It's the way the theatre has chosen to present the author.

There are no fewer than seven pictures of Schwab, most of them full page portraits; Werner checking his quiff in the bathroom mirror of a Graz nightclub; Werner greeting fans at an exhibition of his graphic works; Werner walking down the street trailing a flaming cape behind him, the literal embodiment of a sign saying "Vienna's hotttest stretch of pavement." And he can write, too, it seems: Schwab is explicitly compared with Büchner, Rimbaud, Georg Trakl and Hervé Guibert. These are images of the author as hero. The author as star. The author as (quiz question: what do Büchner, Rimbaud, Trakl, Guibert and Schwab all have in common?) genius who died tragically young.

Despite this early death (another of the photos shows a grave covered by a couple of skipfuls of flowers) you definitely get the impression that Werner's was a job worth having. It wasn't always like this for playwrights in the German-speaking theatre. Six years before *Die Präsidentinnen* opened at the Burgtheater, five and a half before his unfortunate demise following an excess of New Year's Eve celebrations, the unknown Werner Schwab had sent exactly the same play to exactly the same theatre politely offering them the rights to its first performance. The script lay around for 18 months before anyone in the theatre could be bothered to read it and when some anonymous person finally did so, an eight line report reveals that they were less than impressed. "Much unintended humour as a result of the author's lack of linguistic competence... Unperformable." A rejection letter followed a couple of weeks later, just in time to wish Schwab all the best for the New Year, which would be the first of the Nineties.

In fact Schwab was to have a very good year, followed by three even better ones. *Die Präsidentinnen* was performed at the small Künstlerhaus in Vienna, his next play was performed at the larger Schauspielhaus and the one after that at the prestigious Kammerspiele in Munich. This play, *Volksvernichtung oder Meine Leber ist Sinnlos* (*Kill the Poor or My Liver is Meaningless*), was invited to the Theatertreffen in Berlin as one of the 10 best productions in the German speaking theatre that year and to the Mülheim playwriting festival, where it won first prize. Schwab was named young playwright of the year by Theater Heute magazine. More productions, translations and new commissions followed. Suddenly it seemed as if every big player in the highly competitive German-speaking theatre had to have at least one Schwab play in the repertoire.

The speed and extent of Schwab's rise was spectacular, and it revealed that these theatres needed living writers more than they might previously have known. Traditionally, the large state and city theatres in Germany, Austria and German-speaking Switzerland have been built around actors. They have permanent companies and the actors in these companies require parts. If a new play cannot be cast from the company, this is a problem for the play. If there's an empty production slot, it's much easier for these theatres to do an old play which has parts for the actors who need parts or put them all in a room and let them make up a play themselves than to recruit and pay new actors for a single, untried text. It's a way of working diametrically opposed to that of the Royal Court (or indeed the several other British theatres dedicated to new writing) where they try to find the best play they can first and then look for the best actors who are available to do it.

Werner Schwab's plays suddenly got a new audience into the theatre, an audience that was sick of people speaking in verse, who felt that even 1950 was a very long time ago, and who wanted to be able to have a laugh and use their brains at the same time. Schwab's work makes no great claims for its own social or political agenda. *Die Präsidentinnen*, for example, is quite pathologically domestic in setting, but its heroines are epic adventurers in language, willing to fight by any means necessary to support their own story, which is more than just their view of the world, it's their utopia. And here is where Schwab's brilliance and originality lies. There's a deliberate contrast between a very narrow and restricted milieu and an attitude in the writing which is much more permissive and anarchic. The joy of the play is that this permissive anarchy is something that deep down, the characters ultimately share.

The resonance which Schwab's work had proved that good writers can characterize a new sensibility before other people know that's what it is. And as a result, a number of larger theatres suddenly became curious about what other writers there might be out there. If I've devoted rather a lot of this introduction to Werner Schwab, it's because the phenomenon of his career has helped to alter the rules of engagement between playwrights writing in German and the theatres which present their work. Schwab knocked down a door, through which successive waves of other writers have since poured.

So much so, that when Elyse Dodgson of the Royal Court asked me in 1997 to help choose four German-language plays to be translated for a series of readings, my first reaction was to wonder whether four plays would be enough to reflect the quality and diversity of current playwriting in German. This is a lively and exciting time for new German drama. Not only are there more premieres and more theatres are launching sustained commissioning programmes, each recent year has seen the appearance of a number of talented newcomers. In previous years I might have been concerned about the difficulty of finding four plays which I felt would genuinely speak to a London audience. This time I was more worried about whom or what we might have to leave out.

In the end we left out Lothar Trolle and Roland Schimmelpfennig, Thomas Jonigk and Kerstin Specht, Albert Ostermaier, René Pollesch, Lisa Engel and Werner Fritsch. There wasn't room for John von Düffel or Kerstin Hensel or Daniel Call. Anna Langhoff, Klaus Chatten and Dea Loher had all had readings at the Royal Court and had been published in Britain, so we felt less bad about them missing out this time. Wilfried Happel, Helmut Krausser, Jens Roselt and Moritz Rinke didn't make it either. But then we left out Botho Strauss and Tankred Dorst and a whole host of more senior writers: Elfriede Jellinek, Peter Handke, Gerlind Reinshagen, Einar Schleef. Each of these writers had their advocates. And they're all still writing.

In the face of such a dense literary landscape it would be a bit silly of me to try to claim that our eventual selection has managed to include everything that might possibly be of interest. And I'll spare you any theories I might have on how this selection differs collectively from the plays by Klaus Pohl, Dea Loher, Anna Langhoff and D.Rust published in the first volume of German Plays because anyone who wants to can read those plays and make those comparisons for themselves.

What I will say though is that as far as I'm concerned, each of the plays in this book is here on merit. If you don't know any of them you're in for a treat. Oliver Bukowski's *'Til Denver* (translated here by David Spencer as *Jamaica*) is a split-your-sides comedy with an achingly painful heart. Its heroes are two economically unviable, alcoholically incapacitated East Germans whose best years are behind them. The plot revolves around an accidental death and scam kidnapping which they carry out with breathtaking incompetence. What makes these characters utterly lovable is the fighting spirit with which they take on the German language with a hardcore local dialect that is contrasted against the flat, standard German of the wealthy middle-class couple they would like to swindle. For Bukowski, like some Cicero of the long-term unemployed, to speak well is to live well, and Pasch and Ackers both speak brilliantly. David Spencer has made a virtuoso job of translating Bukowski's Niederlausitz dialect into heavy-duty Yorkshire. If you have any trouble following it, all I can say is that it's reader-friendly compared to the original.

Die Lügen der Papagaien (*Parrots' Lies*) by Andreas Marber is a German play whose german-ness evaporates in performance. A great pleasure of the reading which Fiona Shaw directed was that the audience turned up expecting to see a play from another culture and what they got was a play which was set in the Royal Court Theatre. In fact *Die Lügen der Papagaien* has a number of similarities with *'Til Denver* and *Die Präsidentinnen*: small cast, confined setting, distinctive argot and intense conflict. Marber's great coup, though, is that he doesn't just use the theatre to show a bitter conflict in a confined milieu, he chooses the theatre itself as that location and not just any theatre, but the theatre where the play is being performed. His play rigorously exposes all the vanities and self-deceptions lurking in the theatremaking process, the emotional vicissitudes of trying to make a living out of being an artist. Each of the three individuals' motives for being involved are deeply compromised. The play which is being rehearsed has been written purely out of spite. And yet in Marber's play the theatre and acting triumph. Despite what's there on the surface, *Die Lügen der Papagaien* is a glorious and impassioned love letter to the acting profession.

Malaria by Simone Schneider (translated here by Penny Black) is different again. It describes itself as a farce and its form owes a certain amount to *Alice in Wonderland* but as well as being the story of a girl called Isa who meets a boy called Dionysos and falls down a hole with him, the play also functions on a wider metaphorical level, as the portrait of a city, Berlin, stuck in the middle of the biggest make-over of our times. Schneider explores this broader canvas in a manner which is light and playful rather than didactic. The world of *Malaria* is a rich and densely imagined world, the product of an imagination sufficiently suspicious of itself to imagine an entire city in the grip of a mysterious fever of which no one knows the cause or cure: a world to enjoy getting lost in.

In describing the contents of this volume as German plays, I'd suggest that the word 'plays' is considerably more useful than the word 'German'. Anyone reading this book expecting it to provide a realistic portrait of contemporary Germany, Austria and Switzerland is liable to end up confused and disappointed.

If, on the other hand, you read it as a guidebook to what might happen on stage, you can have a lot of fun. These are terrific plays which deserve (and have found) audiences well beyond their native language. Read them out loud. Share them with other people. Let them make you laugh. Let them offer you the unexpected.

David Tushingham
October 1999

HOLY MOTHERS

(*Die Präsidentinnen*)

by Werner Schwab

translated by Meredith Oakes

Werner Schwab was born in Graz, Austria, in 1958 and died in 1994. In 1992 he was elected playwright of the year by German-speaking theatre critics. He wrote over a dozen plays which include *Die Präsidentinnen* (1990), *Übergewicht, unwichtig: Unform* (1991), *Messalliance* (1992), *Pornogeographie* (1993), *Faust:: Mein Brustkorb: Mein Helm* (1994). He wrote two novels: *Abfall, Bergland, Cäsar* (1993) and *Der Dreck und das Gute* published in 1995.

Holy Mothers (*Die Präsidentinnen*) was first performed in English as a reading as part of the *New German Voices* season at the Theatre Upstairs on 3 December 1997 with the following cast:

GRETE	Eleanor Bron
ERNA	Freda Dowie
MARIEDL	Liz Smith

Director Lindsay Posner
Translator Meredith Oakes

Holy Mothers was given its first full performance at the New Ambassadors Theatre on 27 May 1999. It was jointly produced by the Royal Court Theatre, Ambassadors Theatre Group, Guy Chapman and Mark Goucher, with the following cast:

ERNA	Valerie Lilley
GRETE	Paola Dionisotti
MARIEDL	Linda Dobell

Director Richard Jones
Designer Stewart Laing
Lighting Pat Collins
Translator Meredith Oakes

Characters

ERNA, *on a state minimum pension. Apron, orthopaedic shoes, a big grotesque fur bonnet*

GRETE, *pensioner. Quite fat, beehive hairstyle (blonde), tastelessly dressed, lots of cheap jewellery, heavy make-up*

MARIEDL, *dressed like a pauper, hair pulled back, feet stuck into far-too-big hiking boots. She seems a bit simple at first. She is somewhat younger than the other two, and this should be seen in her rather hectic movements*

THE ORIGINAL BREECH-LOADING SOUL SOOTHERS, *in the third scene*

The Set
A small kitchen/living room centre stage. Left and right, complete blackness. The kitchen/living room is lined to the ceiling with junk (photos, souvenirs, religious kitsch, framed calendar pictures, containers etc) but is clean and tidy. There is a museum-like feel to the arrangement of the objects. A small non-naturalistic space therefore, nonetheless recognizable as a lower-middle-class kitchen/living room.

The Language
The language the women create is what they are. It is work to create (elucidate) yourself, so everything is, by its very nature, resistance. This should be perceptible as effort in the play.

The play concerns the fact that the earth is flat, and that the sun rises and sets because it revolves around the earth; it concerns the fact that nothing is willing to be function, only distraction.

Scene One

While the audience take their seats, a broadcast is heard of the Pope celebrating mass with a multitude. The telecast ends and the curtain rises.

ERNA*'s grotesque kitchen/living room.* ERNA *turns off the TV.* MARIEDL *is looking for something under the table.* GRETE *is seated at the table.*

ERNA. All those people. All those people coming together and being together and being all as one at the feet of the Holy Father.

GRETE. And isn't the picture wonderful. The colours could have come from life itself.

ERNA. It's tremendously moving, the sense of peace arising out of all those people. Peace is life's goal, and life is people's goal.

GRETE (*lifts the tablecloth and speaks to someone under the table*). Leave the button, Mariedl, I'm really not that bothered about the button. Forget about the button, sit with us. (*To* ERNA.) It's really clever of you, Erna, to have got yourself that lovely fur bonnet, and the colour television. At last you've brought some enjoyment into your home. Now's the time you should open up to life, and give life the chance to make you happy.

ERNA. Yes, those words slip out so easily, but in reality, enjoying life is very hard, when you've saved and saved, until it's right down in your bones. Still perhaps just for once in my life, happiness will find a person like me, who's never done anything except clean other people's filth. (ERNA *stands before the mirror.*) I found this fur bonnet a year ago, in the rubbish. It's unthinkable that someone would have simply thrown this bonnet away, it's much too valuable. Ob viously it must have been young people, venting their malice on this bonnet. (*She turns her back to the mirror and sits down.*) But you wouldn't believe how filthy it was. I was three and a half hours slaving over it, before it was fit to be taken to the police. (GRETE *gestures that she wants to feel the fur of the hat.* ERNA *bends down to make it easier for her.*) And now a year's gone by and no-one's claimed it. And he was such a nice policeman at the lost property office, he said to me: The reason you're poor is that you're an honest woman. Why not put this bonnet under your Christmas tree, give a little present to yourself for once . . . I try not to indulge myself in general, but I have to admit, I was truly pleased by that.

GRETE. You shouldn't persist with this dreadful saving, you're not as poor as you used to be, Erna. And life goes on, you know, it goes on faster than we can imagine.

ERNA. So now I've allowed myself the television, though the television is a used television of course. It's my one gift to myself in return for all I've given. In every other respect I've always had to save on everything in my life, including my child, Herrmann. If you really know how to save, your life can be planned. Everything can be saved on. Instead of coffee filters, for instance, you can take a bit of toilet paper, and instead of toilet paper, you can use newspaper, which can be picked up from the stairwell, where the papers are left out for recycling – Actually as far as I'm concerned, I could just as well do without the coffee altogether, because luckily I can't digest coffee. But Herrmann refuses to eat his roll and liver sausage without a black coffee to flush it down, as he says. The way he says it, it's as if his roll and liver sausage were human excrement and his stomach were the toilet.

MARIEDL (*under the table*). I don't think it's right, Erna, the way you keep saving. You save far too much, you take it much too far. God doesn't want good people to suffer.

ERNA (*furious, lifts up the tablecloth*). It's easy for you to talk, Mariedl dear, but you live alone and there's never been anyone in your life, has there. You travel the world just as you like, in your spare time. You've already been to Lourdes twice this year, and to Medjugorje, and twice to Mariazell. You don't have the responsibility of an uncontrollable child.

GRETE. But your Herrmann is a man, a manly man.

MARIEDL *appears, sits down, shrugs her shoulders as if not knowing what to do, and begins rhythmically rocking the upper part of her body back and forth.*

ERNA. Yes, he's the picture of a man. Women all turn their heads to look at him, shameless as they are these days. But Herrmann cannot accept anything in this life which is good, or which makes any sense. Up there, I say to Herrmann, up there is where the pictures of my grandchildren will go. (*She points to two white rectangular spaces on the wall.*) But he refuses to do me the honour, he's not going to make any grandchildren. I was keeping five little places free up there, waiting for grandchildren. I've only just now put something else up in three of them, so as not to frighten him. And yet it ought to be so easy, in today's world, for him to have intercourse. People today have intercourse all day. And Herrmann admits, he could have intercourse any time, but he purposely never does have intercourse, because intercourse might actually lead to a pregnancy, which ultimately might lead to a grandchild.

GRETE. Oh stop it, Erna, your Herrmann is so big and strong. Miss Right will find him in the end.

ERNA. Yes that's my one hope, if I have to go on living, my one hope is that God will do something about Herrmann. (*Weepily.*) He does get about a lot, as a sales representative, something might happen, but then he keeps sending me these dreadful postcards, on the front is a beautiful landscape, and on the back he writes, that once again he's had the opportunity of having intercourse, and once again he's made a point of not having intercourse. (*Weeps.*)

GRETE (*pats ERNA on the back to calm her*). But Erna, when Miss Right comes along, she'll just snap up your Herrmann and kiss him. And intercourse will follow by itself. (*She sings.*) Some enchanted evening, You may see a stranger, you may . . . (*Stops suddenly.*) But who on earth am I to talk, look at my fate, Erna, at least Herrmann thinks of you and always sends you one of these cards about intercourse, but what about me? My daughter migrated to Australia nine years ago, and even before that, she got herself gutted like a chicken, ovaries, the lot, everything you need for grandchildren. In nine years she's sent me one postcard. Safely arrived and I'm absolutely fine. She wrote me that eight and a half years ago. Lydia is all I have now.

ERNA. But Herrmann shouldn't keep sending me those cards, all about how he's giving up intercourse for good, or having a vasectomy.

GRETE. Yes, Hannelore, my daughter, and besides, she'll be an old bag by now, she'll be getting on for forty by now. But she's always had peculiar ways, a bit like your Herrmann really. Also Hannelore frequently used to forget that she wasn't the daughter of scum. She often behaved as if she'd had no upbringing. She'd smash her face through a window, then calmly eat the broken glass, and then she'd laugh her head off, cutting her face and her bosom. And if I said to her: Well Lore, at least you look like sliced pork now, the men will want you now; well then she'd just go quiet, and suck her thumb, and sleep thirty hours at a time.

ERNA. Yes that is human life. You try your whole life long to steer a proper course through life, then your own flesh and blood turn their backs on all of it, life, humanity, all of it.

GRETE. Anyway I hope Hannelore will find happiness out there in Australia, if that's how it has to be, with or without the ovaries.

ERNA. Herrmann is so introverted. When he sees a human being, he has to drink a brandy and smoke a cigarette straight away, he says if he doesn't, he'll get eye cancer. Herrmann has a horror of all human beings, and that's why he became a sales representative, in order to meet people, so that every day he's got the perfect excuse for coming home drunk.

MARIEDL. Very many saints have come from people like that, in the time of their youth they hid their face from the world.

ERNA. The time of their youth? But Herrmann's nearly forty.

MARIEDL. Yes but any day we can feel an inner push, and pop goes the button.

ERNA. One little button going pop wouldn't make much difference to Herrmann. It would take a whole button factory exploding. Even he can't even stand himself. When he's washing his face at the tap I have to hang the hand towel over the mirror before he'll go in there. He cuts off half his face when he's shaving, because he won't have a mirror, he says a mirror's disgusting. He says he'll be walking down the street, and the shop windows will start reflecting, so that Herrmann sees Herrmann, and then he throws up on the spot, unless he's drunk. And this is what he's telling me day in day out, and every word he says and every drink he takes, he's shortening my life.

MARIEDL. Those very people are often found by Jesus, or by the Virgin Mary full of grace, the Lord be with you. And from one day to the next grace will suddenly burst from a sick heart. Just as Saul became Paul, Herrmann could become His man.

ERNA. Yes that's the very best thing I could hope for, that inside Herrmann everything could be changed utterly. But what can be expected from someone who all day every day turns his back on everything that makes life worth living. And if I try to say a few good words to him, he laughs, and has a shot of bitters or a shot of brandy.

GRETE. People don't understand what life is. When life speaks to people, and gives them good advice, people shake their heads and act like wogs, no understand, no understand, that's all they can say for themselves. My Lydia's not like that, she understands everything. If I see her eat some strange piece of shit, I say to her, Lydi, don't eat shit. And straight away she lifts up her little head and nods at me. She saw a wooden dachshund do that once, she learned it straight off.

MARIEDL (*enchanted*). Is that really true?

GRETE. Yes, it was a little dachshund on wheels, it had a child with it. You pulled on its lead and it wagged its little tail, and its little head went yesyes, up and down, yesyesyesyesyes.

(GRETE *nods vigorously,* MARIEDL *laughs hysterically.*) It was beautifully painted wood, that little dachshund, and exactly the same size as Lydi, and oh she did like him. And ever since then, she'll nod her head just like him, whenever I say: Lydi, don't eat shit. (MARIEDL *again bursts out laughing, and puts her hands over her mouth.*)

ERNA. That's enough, Grete, I'm not going to listen to any more of your language. You're always entertaining common words on your lips. All we ever hear from you is shit, shit, shit. There are other things people can say, you can say stool, or number two, not this shit, shit, shit all the time.

GRETE. You criticize everything, you always find fault with everything, you spend your whole life pulling everyone down. Then you ask why Hermann won't have intercourse.

ERNA (*somewhat subdued*). But life isn't worth living, is it, if whatever it is you're looking at, suddenly there's a stinking stool next to it. So often it will be one of the few really beautiful things in life, and then no sooner do you reach out and touch it, than once again you've a heap of shit in your hand.

MARIEDL. I don't mind lower words and I don't actually mind a stool. Because what is it, after all, if you didn't know what it is? All it is, is something warm and soft, when it's fresh. (*She draws herself up proudly.*) People always say, Oh no, the toilet's blocked, quick, fetch Mariedl, she does it without. Because they all know I don't put rubber gloves on, when I'm putting my hand down the toilet. (ERNA *is nearly sick, and turns away.*) They all come to me from all the best houses, whenever a blockage occurs. I go into all the best houses and I'm always treated with kindness wherever I go. And anyway it really doesn't make me sick, when I reach down in the toilet bowl, because I'm offering it up to our Lord Jesus Christ, who died on the cross for us. And the best people in the best houses always say to me, would I like some rubber gloves, because they're beautifully mannered well brought up people. But I always say NO, because if the Lord God created the world, He also created human excrement.

ERNA. My God, Mariedl, you really are a filthy cow, you'll have to forgive me, but don't go on please. It's bad enough people having to defecate, and the wicked feelings they so often have. So many times I've asked myself, why do people have to have a bum. It's not a thing of beauty, is it, a bum, yet people worship them and make graven images of them.

GRETE (*taking no notice of* ERNA). And the best people really come to you, do they, and call on you for help?

MARIEDL. Very rich and very fine people have come to me, and once they even fetched me in a great big car to one such afflicted toilet. But they don't exactly have what you'd call a toilet, it's very nice what they have, it doesn't even smell like a toilet, it smells just the same as rich ladies do. I've been fetched to the toilet twice by the Sunday school teacher, and once by the priest. And the priest solemnly promised he'd spread the word through all the congregation, all about Mariedl and what I can do, so that other people can also call on me to come to them when they have a blockage in their toilet.

ERNA. I don't understand that. My toilet bowl is never blocked. It's because people are so thoughtless, I expect, and put the wrong things down, because it isn't easy to block one of those bowls with a stool on its own. I often do quite a large, hard one, because of worrying about Herrmann which pushes it all together inside me. What you have to do, is give it a firm shove with the toilet brush and flush twice. But of course you mustn't put too much toilet paper down, because then, anything can happen. Herrmann always gets cross with me, when he's just passed a stool, and I'm listening at the door for how many pieces of paper he's tearing off. But I say to him, it's important, first, because it's a chance to save, and second because it's dangerous if the paper gets all mixed up with one of his bad, sticky jobs. But he just laughs, and has another drink.

GRETE (*interested, to* MARIEDL). What things do rich people put down their toilets that obstruct them so dreadfully?

MARIEDL. There was a jam jar once, with red worms in it for the aquarium fish, and a whole chicken another time, but I think it must have been smelly even before they put it down the toilet. Books there have been, with pictures of naked people, and underwear, bloodstained or soiled. (ERNA *is practically being sick*.) Don't look so tragic, Erna, you take everything in life so seriously. Life is honest, that's all, and shows people what we consist of. Once you've reached down a toilet bowl, soon all your dreadful fears have gone, and then it's just the same as shaking someone's hand. (ERNA *is nearly sick*.)

GRETE. When it's Lydia's jobs it never bothers me either, because I always know exactly what she's eaten. But people today eat all kinds of things, with all the rich food available. Even the lowest types can purchase anything they fancy.

ERNA. I couldn't do it. I simply couldn't. It would simply make me throw up. I'd heave my guts out. I retch when I so much as brush my teeth. And then when Herrmann sees me brushing my teeth and retching, he pretends to retch as well. He deliberately imitates those inevitable human sounds of someone retching. And he deliberately fools about for so long, pretending he's retching, that finally up comes all his roll and liver sausage. And then do you know what he says to me, the sod, he says to me, you see mum, I told you I don't like liver sausage.

GRETE. Nonsense Erna, why do you have to live in this state of perpetual exaggeration. Herrmann's a big fine man, a marvellous figure of a man, and that's the truth, all he needs is the right woman. If I were a young girl today – well who knows what might happen, love goes on oiled wheels today. (*Giggles*.)

ERNA. I don't know, Grete, I really don't, conversing with you it always comes back to sex or heaps of shit. I simply cannot reconcile my belief in God with sex and a little heap of shit. Don't think badly of me if I say this, but our Grete's always been a naughty girl, haven't you. After all, you've been married twice, and your front door hasn't always shut properly either, when it should have.

GRETE. Why should I have to like whatever your dirty mind dumps on the table in front of me, Erna. I was only having these thoughts about Herrmann because when I'm at my window, watching to see the pigeons don't eat the birds' food, I often catch sight of him down in the street . . .

MARIEDL. What have you got against pigeons? Pigeons are heaven's creatures too.

GRETE. Oh come on Mariedl, really . . . (*Makes a cuckoo sign at* MARIEDL, *twirling her finger at her temple.*) Anyway when I see Herrmann, all big and blond and blue-eyed, I often think what a nice ambience Herrmann's got. Hermann sets me off remembering the sins of my youth. (*Smiles roguishly.*)

MARIEDL. But why have pigeons got no rights in your birdbox? Pigeons are birds.

GRETE. Oh what's the matter with your brains, Mariedl? What on earth do you know about nature? Pigeons completely destroy a window birdbox. Pigeons eat young tits. Lydi gets worn out by those vermin. You should see what it's like, the pounding of her little heart, when the pigeons have upset her, then you wouldn't talk such rubbish.

ERNA. I believe in every living thing being treated well in this world. I'm the first one to feel the horror, when they show on television all the dreadful things that happen. But it was very good what the Bundespresident said in his latest speech, he said he ranged himself on the side of peace and forgiveness. I always say forgiveness is the most important thing on this earth. I'm always able to forgive Herrmann, for everything. When he's yet again abused his body with alcohol, I always say to him, Herrmann, a mother always forgives. But when I forgive him, he always picks up the bottle and drinks, he doesn't even bother with a glass.

MARIEDL. We must always keep our engine of brotherly love running. Whenever I'm able to help someone, happiness steps in through the door of my heart. And if there's ever a time when nobody's needing Mariedl's busy hands, I sit sadly in my room. I'm not very fond of being in my room, that's why I only need a small room, because I'm not at home in a room. So it's lucky that busy hands with brotherly love in them are needed all over the world. My children are all the people I've been privileged to help. Yes, those are my children, and they're all my friends. When they see Mariedl, they say: Ah, Mariedl, are you off again so soon? She works so hard, everyone likes a person like that, and she does it without. (*Jumps up suddenly and shouts.*) Everyone has a place in their heart for Mariedl, because of her many good deeds –

ERNA. Yes yes, we know what a hard-working soul you are. And you'll get your reward one day. Faith is the only bridge across this valley of tears. But you're making the same mistake as me now, you're taking life too seriously. Not like our Grete, she's been clever with her life, Grete's had her fun.

GRETE (*furious*). Don't you think you're being rather nasty? How can you be so nasty behind that laughing face of yours? Do you think my life has all been one big barrel of laughs? First I was divorced, then I was widowed. Do you think marriage is one great big pleasure trip? What about Kurti, my first husband? And Hannelore? What do you imagine it's like when you know, because you can't help knowing, that your very own husband is punishing your very own daughter in your very own bed? What about that for God's sake?

What you do is, you wait and see, you wait and see what providence has in mind for people. But you have to give providence the space to work, until you finally find out what it's going to be. And at last, when providence is finished, life becomes much less painful. Because what's the use of getting so worked up, you can't change providence, can you. You can't just grab hold of providence by the throat and say to it, make me happy. (*She throttles an imaginary throat.*)

No, and in a way I understand about Kurti and Hannelore. Beautiful memories are so much a part of love. Kurti often said to me, Hannelore's as beautiful now as you were, when you were a girl. Of course it was wrong, what went on there, and anyway Hannelore was too young at that stage. But you have to understand Kurti as well. He was such a handsome officer in the war, he was so proud, and he must have felt, when we had those victories at the beginning, that the whole world was going to belong to someone like him. The whole of the rest of his life he never got rid of that taste he had for victory. And then when Hannelore went off to Australia, he divorced me and married that Chinese or Thailander, whatever she is. I've never understood that, what he could have seen in a slit-eyed eighteen-year-old.

ERNA. The physical is mankind's tragedy. Even good people are often completely destroyed by lust. When you're young, and the world breaks in on your humanity with its physicality, as often as not it's the physicality that drives the humanity out of the world.

GRETE. Yes, and because life brings all these experiences along with it, I've totally turned my back on love now, though I still have opportunities. These days, and with a light heart, Grete just says NO . . . And if those old warm feelings still occasionally come up, I go out and buy myself a hot dog and a piece of emmenthal, and a gherkin and a small bottle of beer, and life soon smiles again.

ERNA. You can make wonderful savings on food. I'll tell you who's cheap – Wottila. He has liver sausage on permanent special offer. There's nowhere you can buy liver sausage as cheap as at Karl Wottila. I can't even remember how long it is I've been buying liver sausage from Wottila. Wottila actually told me once, liver sausage has given him a great deal to be thankful for, businesswise, and because of that, all his life he's kept the liver sausage down, pricewise. It's been a kind of a vow with him, he made that quite clear to me. He promised himself that if ever in life he achieved his own butcher's shop, he'd keep the price of liver sausage right down in the basement for a lifetime. Yes, and it came to pass he did achieve his own butcher's shop, and now the people stand in line to obtain their liver sausage cheap. He's also had a very interesting life, Wottila, he was actually born in Poland, he told me all about it, when he was visiting here.

GRETE. Did Wottila come and visit you?

ERNA. Very much so, and he brought me some flowers and a kilo of mince.

MARIEDL. Wottila is a very religious man. Wottila has a very strong faith.

GRETE. Erna, Erna, he's the one for you, even if he is a Pole. But a non-smoker, Erna, and he's teetotal. Might he not be visiting you again?

ERNA (*weepily*). We were sitting right here, in this very spot, talking together, it was beautiful, everything we said was so full of meaning. Then Herrmann, the sod, came into the room, he'd just finished sleeping it off, and he says, aha, aha, and he's making sniffing actions, aha, he says, what's that stink of liver sausage, quick, I need a drink – I was so ashamed, I was sitting there wishing the ground would swallow me up. But Wottila kept very calm, all he said was, he didn't think from the look of him that Herrmann was ever likely to gain eternal salvation. He said you could see it straight away from Herrmann's face, he said there wasn't enough matter in it, and no eternal flame would light up in his head.

GRETE. Go on Erna, you don't have to believe everything Wottila says.

ERNA. Wottila's had years of experience. That's his hobby, he studies the faces of all his meat customers. He told me once I'm a good woman but I've got an unhappy life, and that was exactly right.

MARIEDL. We should never ever give up on someone. We should always stay with them, and try to shepherd them with foresight and hindsight in the direction of faith, that's what the priest said.

ERNA. Wottila's a strict man, because he lives alone. Anyway I said to him, I can't just push my own son out the door. But also you have to remember that Wottila had a vision once, in the middle of a dark wood, when he came to a clearing. He was just about to light up a cigarette and take a shot of bitters when suddenly the Virgin Mary appeared to him. He got such a shock he fell over backwards. She was ten and a half feet tall and beautifully dressed, and she said to him, smoking and drinking are sins against health, give them up, go back and do penance, and tell this to all the world. After that, Wottila fell into a coma which lasted several hours. And when he came to, he found a bunch of white roses beside him, and a bottle of mineral water. So he created a shrine in that place, and ever since then he's only ever drunk mineral water, perhaps at most a milk coffee in the mornings, but never bitters, never again.

GRETE. That may well be true, but Wottila isn't right about everything. You told me yourself how Wottila once said that Herrmann should eat plenty of liver sausage, on account of his sick alcoholic liver. And that, my dear Erna, is wrong, totally wrong, it's been scientifically proved, I asked a real gynaecologist, my gynaecologist.

ERNA. Scientifically – scientifically, well scientists are unable to agree among themselves, though most believe in God, even Albert Einstein. That's what the priest said. Besides, I don't credit everything the scientists say, it simply doesn't work like that. And don't try and tell me Wottila's liver sausage isn't good for Herrmann's liver, because I refuse to believe it. If you'd seen how Wottila works with sausages, he's so upright and so clean, you can be absolutely sure no uncleanliness would ever get in, and none of those poisonous additives that might harm people. Yes and your gynaecologists can all go and jump in the lake, they can't even think straight, because all they're doing, day in and day out, is dealing in sex.

GRETE. Oh really Erna . . . Really . . . (*Laughs.*) You won't hear a word against Karl Wottila, will you, because you're in love with him, because he's one of the God squad.

MARIEDL (*very loudly*). We don't say God squad.

ERNA (*jumps up*). Yoouu . . . you're a Nazi, you're a divorcee, you're not even allowed to take proper communion.

GRETE (*jumps up*). You're divorced as well, you old bible basher.

ERNA. Yes but I was the innocent party, I can eat the communion.

GRETE. Yeees, because your twat's all wrong, nothing will go in there except a bit of liver sausage.

MARIEDL *begins to cry.*

ERNA. Sex . . . sex, that's all you know. You're a whore, a Nazi Hitler whore.

GRETE. Nazi . . . Nazi, what do you know about Nazis. Everyone was Nazis then. And if I'm a whore, you're a nun with a sewn-up twat.

ERNA (*shouts*). The truth, the truth is, no-one was a Nazi, a handful at most. Not in this country, nooo, that was Hitler, he was evil, he misled people. And that's exactly what our Bundespresident's been saying. But what's the point my talking to someone who doesn't even get herself to church half the time. People who reject the mass are only fit for the meat grinder, that's what Wottila says.

GRETE (*full of hate, steps up to* ERNA). Yees, and what a shame it is, that Hitler never caught up with your Polish liver-sausage bishop back then.

ERNA *shrieks and attacks* GRETE. *They have a long and merciless fight.* MARIEDL *tries to pray out loud but is repeatedly interrupted by her own sobbing. Suddenly, as if turned to stone, the combatants stop. Embarrassed, they loosen their grip on each other and begin to tweak themselves back into shape.* MARIEDL *calms down and picks up the pieces of hair from* GRETE*'s beehive.* ERNA *and* GRETE *sit on the floor completely disorientated. After a while,* ERNA *gets up, and with* MARIEDL*'s help lifts fat* GRETE *to her feet.*

ERNA. What a stupid fuss about nothing.

MARIEDL (*zealously tidying the room*). Now you've got to be friends again, and learn to love thy neighbour again.

GRETE. You should learn to accept other people's opinions, Erna, that's what we have to be able to do, and the Bundespresident said that as well.

ERNA. Yes but so should you.

GRETE. What do you mean? do you think I'm not a Christian? I am a Christian, you know, but it's harder for me than it is for ordinary people. And why? Because of Lydi of course. Am I supposed to leave her all alone, while I go off to mass? That's the problem, don't you see, I've always wanted to say that to you, Erna. And I couldn't expect a bright little thing like Lydi to stay sitting still all that time in the church, even supposing they'd let her in. So what am I supposed to do with Lydi on a Sunday?

ERNA. I can understand it's a real problem, Grete. I really didn't mean it like that.

GRETE. And I didn't mean what I said about Wottila. There's nothing the matter with his liver sausage, even Lydi eats a little bit of it sometimes, and she's very fussy.

MARIEDL. Now brotherly love is back in place. Now you have to kiss each other and it will all be all right again.

She pushes ERNA*'s and* GRETE*'s heads together. At first* GRETE *and* ERNA *are unwilling, then they fall into each other's arms.*

ERNA. Let's put all life's filth out of our minds. The best thing we can do is enjoy ourselves. Herrmann's in the pub, your daughter's in Australia and Mariedl's all right, isn't she. Let's forget all about problems and politics.

GRETE. You're right, why shouldn't a couple of old *Blunzen* like us be having some fun as well. I'll go across and get some wine.

MARIEDL. Just remind me, what is a *Blunze*?

GRETE. A blood sausage.

ERNA. Ha ha, which brings us back to Karl Wottila.

End of Scene One.

Scene Two

Again, ERNA*'s kitchen/living room. The arrangement is still the same but the space looks somehow different. Its social characteristics have become blurred, and have taken on a more festive character, more like the atmosphere of a fairground. On the table is a small open wine bottle with three exceedingly large glasses and a breadbasket with dry rolls. The TV is on and shows the test pattern. Everyone is comfortable and sipping the wine.*

ERNA. I can say to him a hundred times, come and sit down Herrman and watch the film, it has a meaning, it will be good for your conscience. But he purposely won't watch the film.

MARIEDL. Films are nearly all beautiful. The mountains and the sea, and people kiss each other on the mouth and have real babies. And there are always very difficult difficulties, which are transported out of the world by the good people.

ERNA. A good film shows life as it could be, if people would only be kind to one another. It's important to show good people in films, in order to make people kinder, especially the young towards the old.

GRETE. And above all, a film has to have some fun in it, to give life a bit of relaxation.

ERNA. Yes daily life needs a little relief. But I also like a problem film with a meaning, because of the cross I bear like a punishment in life because of Herrmann –

MARIEDL. Cheerfulness is fertilizer for the soul, if it's tasteful. The priest says, the shepherd loves his sheep when they frolic.

GRETE (*raises her glass*). Cheers! (*Sings.*) 'Roll out the barrel, we'll have a barrel of fun . . . '

ERNA (*laughs*). You do make me laugh, Grete, you've really got the art of entertainment in your nature. It's another thing we must to be able to do, is have a good time. But you're not as oppressed by your missing child, as I am with Herrmann.

GRETE. We're not having any more Herrmann sagas. (*Sings.*) 'Did you think I'd cry, Did you think I'd lay down and die,

Oh no not I etc . . . ' (MARIEDL *applauds rapturously.*)

ERNA (*mildly*). Don't make fun of me, Grete.

GRETE. Yes but we're celebrating aren't we for once, the hat, and the colour television, so that's enough – (*To* MARIEDL.) Come on Mariedl, sing us a happy song.

MARIEDL (*thinks. Sings*). 'My ding-a-ling, my ding-a-ling, having such fun with my ding-a-ling . . . '

ERNA. Well I never . . .

MARIEDL *falls silent,* ERNA *and* GRETE *look at her astonished. Suddenly* GRETE *starts laughing and shrieking.*

GRETE. She doesn't know what she's singing, hahaha . . .

ERNA. You shouldn't always think the worst Grete, it's a popular song that's all.

GRETE. Well what would you say is meant by a ding-a-ling. You're not as loopy as her.

ERNA. Yes but you shouldn't be taking it on such a vulgar level, it's intended to be symbolic, that's the level it's meant on.

MARIEDL *understanding nothing of this, shakes her head in bewilderment.*

GRETE. Rubbish, when I say something, I say it, and when I celebrate something, I celebrate it. My inner self is thinking back to the times when Grete still used to be in love. And my inner self is celebrating, with a glass of wine.

MARIEDL. Mariedl can always tell when the hearts of others are swelling up and bouncing like a rubber ball. (*She stands up and tries out a couple of dance steps, but immediately sits down again.*)

ERNA. The most I allow myself to think is, that one day, Wottila and I might go to Rome. An urbi et orbi in St Peter's square, that would be wonderful, or even just a trip into the countryside – or a nice party perhaps.

GRETE. Yes. A nice big beerfest would be just the thing for Grete. With lots of people and musicians, all in magnificent costumes. There'd be one musician who's especially big and strong, a handsome devil, he's so powerful, he plays the tuba. And he's winking at me the whole time, what a cheek. You can see straight away he's the biggest rogue out of all those musicians, because he's the only one that's got his sleeves rolled up. And when there's a lull in the music, this handsome one drinks beer out of a huge great tankard and he raises it to Grete. And Grete takes hold of her wineglass and raises that a little bit as well. And without any of the festive gathering being aware of it, there's now been established a line of communication between the stage, where the musicians are, and the little table where Grete is sitting. And suppose there's now a longer pause in the music, and someone gets up on the stage and starts telling jokes. The handsome one, he's called Freddy, now has plenty of time in which to observe Grete. But Grete only looks at him a little bit, because she isn't one of those women who'll be standing there in their combinations the minute a man shows an interest. Nevertheless, Grete can feel how love has come in the door and is taking hold of her and Freddy.

MARIEDL. Mariedl's allowed to help out behind the bar, at the party. She's ever so busy wiping everything clean, and sometimes she's allowed to serve someone. Admiring eyes are watching Mariedl's skilful hands whisking about with the dishcloth. Suddenly a well dressed man bursts into the party in a terrible state, and tells all the people enjoying themselves that the toilet is blocked, that all the toilets are blocked, and that human excrement is already rising to the edge of the toilet bowls.

ERNA. Everyone's allowed to enjoy themselves for now, because the soul has to have a break. But before the party, all the good people have been to mass, because you should give thanks to God before embarking on a good time and a bit of fun. Wottila's forehead is still wet with the holy water, when he arrives at the party with Erna on his arm. And everyone's holding alcoholic drinks under Wottila's nose, and unhealthy cigarettes. But all he says, he says, Think, turn back, and tell this to all the world. And Erna looks up at him, happily.

All three women fantasize intermittently with their eyes closed and their heads laid back.

GRETE. Meanwhile Freddy's been playing the tuba so hard, he's carved out some free time. He signals to the other musicians, they're all attractive, to change round their music to something without any tuba in it, because he might not have much time to play the tuba now. (*Giggles.*)

MARIEDL. Everyone's been drinking lots of good beer, and eating lots of good meat, and soon they all feel an urge, a terrific urge, because food desires to depart from the human body, once the nourishment has been drawn from it. But what can they do, everything is blocked, there isn't a single toilet they can use. Also the tension is mounting, because one toilet has already overflowed. People are all brandishing their arms and shouting, Where's Mariedl, she does it without; fetch Mariedl, because the toilet has yet to be blocked that could withstand her.

ERNA. And Erna playfully drinks a glass of wine, and Wottila eyes her in quite a roguish way.

GRETE. Freddy is smiling in definitely a roguish way, but he's very embarrassed. Because he's just got up his courage to come and sit next to Grete. Grete looks at him out the corner of her eyes and she sees poor Freddy has gone red right up to the roots of his blond hair. Lydi barks out loud under Grete's table, because she's extremely jealous. (*Laughs.*) But Freddy puts his head down under the table and strokes Lydi so delicately, she falls for him as well.

MARIEDL. Mariedl has been discovered among the crowd. Everyone drinks a toast to Mariedl. Hurrah, hurrah, hurrah comes the cheer and they carry her on their shoulders to the toilet. The priest is already there and he's got a roguish smile as well, he's got a new pair of pink rubber gloves in his hand and he's waving them in Mariedl's face. But Mariedl just shakes her head. Then everybody laughs, because they already knew Mariedl would shake her head. And the whole crowd steps aside so Mariedl can get to work. She's already taking off her green waistcoat and rolling up the sleeves of her pink blouse above the elbows.

ERNA. Yes but meanwhile Erna is eating a smoked meat roll with gherkins which Wottila has bought for her. When Wottila went over to the bar, he sniffed the smoked meat rolls and he said the smoked meat wasn't really proper, not like in his shop. But he said it was better than nothing, and a person shouldn't be fussy. Anyway it tastes good enough to Erna because she's having such a wonderful time, and Wottila looks down, quite human, and he even says perhaps they might have a dance when there's a slow tune.

GRETE. And that Freddy, oh he really can dance. He takes tight hold of Grete and whirls her about underneath the decorations. He knows just what to do, being a musician, but the other girls, with their spotty boys, keep on watching him. And the things he keeps saying in Grete's ear, now it's her turn to blush. And he's already felt her once down there. But poor Lydi. Just for the moment Grete's had to tie her up – outside the room because of the noise. And she's so brave . . . no barkies, just a little whimper.

MARIEDL. Mariedl is in the midst of her work, but she hasn't found anything yet. There's something deep down which is causing the blockage, and also people have done such a lot of firm hard stools in there, they keep coming to the surface one after another. But then Mariedl feels a thing which is even harder. It's hard and smooth and sort of round. So she manages to get her fingers round it and it's a tin, and what's more, a tin which hasn't been opened. And all the people are applauding as Mariedl holds up the tin in her hands and the water rushes down the toilet. Then the priest says that now the tin belongs to Mariedl, and he throws her a tin opener. He says to her to look for the good which may be inside. Quick as a flash, she's wiped the poo off the tin and it's neatly opened. And there in the open tin is a goulasch, and oh it does smell good. And the priest says, it's a Hungarian goulasch, a spicy one, and with that, he throws Mariedl a fork and a bread roll.

GRETE. Yes, it's poor Lydi just for now, but little does she know how unbelievably happy she soon will be. Freddy's been feeling Grete more and more, and in addition, he himself is getting quite big inside his trousers. He's been

telling Grete all about how he owns a big farm, with lots of
people working for him and it's even got its own
slaughterhouse. There'll be lots of room for Lydi to be let
out, and all the best meat. And he says how Grete would be
just the kind of a live wire to be the boss's wife. And Grete
can see very clearly that providence is in the process of
bringing about exactly the right thing for her. Freddy says
to Grete, why don't they go outside and find a quiet spot
somewhere. But Grete wags her finger at him and gets a
little bit cross. And she says to him, she's serious about him,
it's not that she doesn't understand what he's saying, but
there's a proper way of doing things. And Freddy-baby
respects her for that. You're a woman for life, he says, and
he's right. I actually say to him, When you're right, you're
right. And he gets even bigger inside his trousers.

MARIEDL. Mariedl dips half her bread roll in her tin of
goulasch and . . .

ERNA. Hang on, not yet. (*She glares at* MARIEDL.) It's a
slow tune, can't you hear it? (*She lifts her head dreamily.*)
At last they're playing something slow . . . Wottila takes
Erna's elbow, and asks if he can have the honour. He tells
her straight away, he's not much of a dancer, what with
being a godfearing person and having worked himself up to
his own butcher's shop, he's never really had the time to
shake a leg. And he even laughs a little bit, and says that if
you want to make something of your life, you have to watch
every step and watch every mouthful, he says. And Erna
knows just what he means, she knows what life is like when
you have to save, and her heart grows very soft. And as
they're playing the final chords, Wottila says very quietly in
Erna's ear, that he has to go into the toilets, because his
braces have come undone at the back and he has to fix
them, and he might avail himself of the facilities to pass a
stool while he's there. Yes, says Wottila, it's a hard life, a
bachelor's life. Which goes to show how much trust he's
already come to place in Erna, the fact that he can tell her
an intimate thing like that.

MARIEDL. Yes, and Mr Karl Wottila is welcome to come,
because Mariedl has already unblocked one toilet. And now

she's got her strength back, thanks to the goulasch. That's the first time it's ever happened to Mariedl that a toilet has turned out to be blocked with something edible. There are people standing in a circle all around her, a couple of metres back, which is understandable, because they're put off by the smell. But they don't begrudge her the delicious goulasch, you can see that, because of the way everyone is smiling. And now she's finished the goulasch, they're all calling out go, go, go, and cheering her on to the next toilet. And the priest's already standing there laughing ever so roguishly, and waving the rubber gloves. And all the happy people are calling out all at once, Mariedl does it without, Mariedl does it without . . . And already Mariedl is thrusting her hand deep into the toilet, she knows what to do, Mariedl does. In no time at all, she's fished out the sodden toilet paper and all the soft stool, and once again, she feels something hard . . . It feels like glass, she says to herself, and whoosh, up it comes, and once again the water's rushing down the toilet, it's a joy to hear it, and what has Mariedl got in her hand? It's a bottle of beer, a full bottle of beer, and once again, it hasn't been opened. The perfect thing with goulasch, thank you father, she says, because now she understands exactly what's going on, the priest wanted to give her a surprise, and he's done just like the easter bunny and hidden a little present in the toilet, a lovely bottle of Styrian beer. And now Mariedl knows why the third toilet is blocked. Because probably that naughty priest has put something down that one as well. I'm really curious to know what's hidden in the third toilet.

ERNA. Yes but now it's time to give Mariedl's toilet a rest, at last, because an honest man like Wottila deserves to have his say as well.

GRETE. What about Freddy? What's he supposed to do with his hard-on, pickle it? Wottila is sitting on the toilet which Mariedl's made available. So it's Freddy now, and Grete.

GRETE *closes her eyes and smiles dreamily.* ERNA *shakes her fist at* GRETE *and glares at her for a long time, full of hatred.* MARIEDL *happily drinks an imaginary bottle of beer.*

GRETE. Now where was I, the finger. Grete wags her finger at Freddy, just as if he were a little boy, and what does he do, the rogue? He shows a finger to her as well, but it's his finger. And Freddy has a big round forefinger, and what does that rogue do with it? No sooner has he waltzed Grete out of the spotlight than he puts that finger up Grete's privates. And it gives her such a thrill, but she has to bring her darling back to earth again. And Freddy understands her straight away, of course he does, he doesn't want a whore for a wife. So Grete whips out Freddy's finger, and Freddy looks at his finger with an expression of happiness on his face, and presses his lips to it. Yes yes, Grete says to her darling, now you've had your finger in Grete's treasure chest, and it's nothing like the dead chickens you find in some women's underwear, is it. And what does Freddy-baby do? There on the spot, he asks Grete to marry him. But Grete knows her way around, so all she says is, she'd like to dance for a bit, and perhaps later on there'll be an answer that Grete can give to Freddy.

MARIEDL. And the beer is like the elixir of life to Mariedl –

ERNA. Wait a minute, you're not getting away with that. Just shut up, Mariedl. Because how could anyone possibly think Wottila would still be on the toilet, there's nothing the matter with his intestines you know. As soon as he gets back he says to me, he did a quick firm stool, because he's not a sick pig like those people that smear filthy words about everything on toilet walls. If anything, he says, the disgusting things written there in that toilet actually made his bowels move all the faster. The Pope, the Bundespresident, everything's dragged through the mud in there, says Wottila, and he even gives Erna a kiss on the nose. But a lot depends on having the proper nourishment of course, he says, bad stools are the result of negligent eating. And people who have bad stools wind up spending a lot of time on the toilet, and then along come the bad thoughts that those kind of people have, who write up all their disgusting filth on toilet walls. Wottila is a very clever man. For instance, he says it would be a good idea to put up a simple cross on the wall facing the toilet, or a photograph

of the Bundespresident, because in schools and public
buildings they have photographs like that. It would remind
people of their own unworthiness, it would make people
remember that they themselves are nothing but little heaps
of shit, and that they shouldn't write on the walls. But what
can you say about a world, he says, where bad substances
have no sooner collected in the human body than they start
trying to immortalize their sickness all over their surround-
ings. Wottila's so right in everything he says, he definitely
has a calling, in fact he's now become a member of the
church council. I'm now responsible for worldly issues and
for the entire development of the church, he says.

MARIEDL *has been listening raptly. During* ERNA*'s
explanation she has moved her chair very close to* ERNA*'s.
Now she pulls it away with a lot of noise and commotion.*

MARIEDL. I'm really glad Mariedl solved all the toilet's
problems, because Mr Karl Wottila is a man who really
inspires respect in people, especially now he's on the church
council . . . (*Reflectively at first, then suddenly bursting out.*)
But not even Mr Church Councillor Wottila knows what
kind of a surprise is hidden in the third toilet. Only God
knows that, and the priest, and perhaps the angels, oh and of
course the Virgin Mary. So there's a huge crowd already
waiting at the third toilet, and they shout their loudest when
strong Mariedl puts her whole arm down the toilet, right to
the armpit hairs. But there was nothing hard or smooth
down in the hole. That's funny, thinks Mariedl, perhaps it
really is just stools blocking the toilet, but then I saw the
priest was laughing really roguishly again and he said I
should reach further down. You are a rascal, Mariedl says to
the priest, and she reaches down again through everything
which is in the toilet bowl. And then she feels such a
strange thing and she pulls it out, and it's a little package
wrapped in a little plastic bag so the pretty wrapping paper
won't get wet in the toilet. And now everyone's clapping
and singing, For she's a jolly good fellow, for she's a jolly
good fellow, for she's a jolly good fellow, and so say all of
us. And the people are overjoyed at seeing Mariedl so happy.
And the priest says the little package is in recognition of all

Mariedl's hard work. Quickly she opens it. And what's inside? It's French perfume, real, so Mariedl can smell nice.

GRETE. A woman like Grete doesn't need perfume, although she gets it all the time as presents from her admirers. But Grete's own body smell is so good already that she practically never uses foreign scents. And Freddy has just said I smell as good as his favourite meal, roast pork and roast potatoes. And that's an important quality in a wife, that she smells at least as good as her husband's favourite meal. But now Grete has a tough decision to make and a huge responsibility: should she give her hand to Freddy for all the rest of her life? She goes a little distance away from the party, so she can talk about it to Lydi, but Lydi's caught up in a terrible conflict of her own. On the one hand, there's all that space to run around in, and the lovely meat, but on the other hand, she's going to have to share her mistress with Freddy. It isn't easy for Lydi, you have to understand that, even though Lydi is so taken with Freddy as well. And while Grete is standing there, with absolutely no idea any more of what decision she should latch on to, all of a sudden Lydi starts nodding her little head saying yesyesyesyesyes. Now Grete knows she can grab hold of Freddy, with God's blessing. And all at once she feels a great surge of happiness in her heart and she walks back into the party with a firm step. Freddy's already coming towards her, and his eyes are electric with suspense and fear, and yearning and desire. He goes down on his knees to her, and he says that if she hits him with a no, he'll kill himself. Oh darling, you great big silly, says Grete running her fingers through his golden hair, I think it's a yes, says Grete. He jumps up as if a wild boar had just bitten him, and would you believe it, he's yelling at the top of his voice, she'll have me, she'll have me, and next minute he's up on the stage. All his musician friends are shaking him by the hand congratulating him on the lovely Grete, and he grabs his tuba and plays on it till it practically explodes. Everyone at the party is happy, and they dance around the handsome young couple. But many of the men are quite dashed, because they wanted Grete for themselves, but Grete's made her choice and she's going to have to send those disappointed men on their way, because she's chosen her one and only, and he's beyond compare. (GRETE *is exhausted and happy, she wipes the sweat off her face*.) Aaah, that was good . . .

MARIEDL. Mariedl opens the bottle of perfume and takes a quick sip . . .

ERNA. I never knew you had such a sewer pipe of a mouth, Mariedl. Can't you see that Erna and Wottila have been sitting closer and closer together? You ought to realise there's something so wonderful happening that it has to be told. (*She lifts her head and becomes dreamy again*.) The two of them are eating another smoked meat roll as well, except that now Erna's having a milk coffee with hers, because another glass of wine might send her feelings stampeding over the edge of the abyss. And besides, Wottila has taken one of Erna's work-roughened hands and is holding it between the two of his, and he's looking with respect at her worn fingers. He says the Mother of God who appeared to him in the clearing strongly resembled Erna, just as she also resembled his mother, except the Mother of God was much more magnificent clotheswise, and had these crazy lighting effects around her. When Erna hears this, she immediately feels as if her inner self is shooting straight up to heaven. I'm honoured, she says, it's all she's capable of saying, she's so overwhelmed. And Wottila says: There has to be a deeper symbolic significance, doesn't there, if my mother and the Mother of God and my best customer, Frau Erna, all look practically the same. I'm going to have to do something about this, thus speaks my soul, he says. Yes, says Erna, but what can we do? Well, possibly, marriage might be a good idea, says Wottila, and also from a business point of view, because a butcher's shop needs a woman's touch, he says. Yes I can understand that, says Erna. Then Wottila takes a deep breath and says: His Will be done, I'm putting my meat business in your hands, Frau Erna Wottila. Frau Erna Wottila, whispers Erna completely overcome. And Wottila solemnly announces: I think we might risk another smoked meat roll and a glass of wine. Yes, says Erna, and with a boiled egg on it this time please. That's two shillings extra, he says, but this day is so special, it's right in its way. And with real distinction in his stride, he goes over to the bar and orders his order.

MARIEDL *puts up her hand like a child in school, while sticking her other finger up her nostril. She is disregarded.*

GRETE. Grete has a great bundle of happiness right now as well. Freddy is totally wild about Grete, he has to keep adjusting his lederhosen, they're squeezing him so tight. But he keeps control of himself like a good boy, because he honours and respects her womanhood. And Grete's always been one who looks to the future, the main thing she's thinking about now is the cut of her wedding dress and what she'll give Lydi for a wedding present. A veal chop, that goes without saying, but there ought to be something special as well. Maybe a new doggie bed.

ERNA. In Erna and Wottila a deep peace has broken out. The two of them can't think of anything else that needs to be said. Erna's feeling a bit sick because of all the smoked meat rolls, but when you've had too many good things to eat for once, it's a pleasant form of sickness. Naturally Erna is thinking of the future to come, because there's a big responsibility lying in wait for her. After all she's changing from a cleaner into a businesswoman, it's a big transition. And she's going to have to be even more careful in everything she does, because her whole life will have gained in importance. When someone's in the business world they can't simply go about with anyone and everyone just as they please, because when the wave of responsiblity hits the deck of the ship of life, then there's all sorts of things you can no longer allow yourself. A businesswoman must keep dirt and filth at arm's length from her life.

MARIEDL *is growing more restless, she's putting her hand up again and scraping at the floor with her mountain boots.*

GRETE. Yes and Grete knows as well that her fastidiousness is going to have to come out even more strongly than before. As mistress of a proper estate you become even more of a target for life's filth. And Lydi has new responsibilities also, she's going to have to become a real watchdog, there'll be no more eating shit, because she's going to have to guard

Grete and Freddy from all the unpleasantnesss of the world. Bad elements come piling in on you, when you move up and make something better of yourself. We're going to need a lot of security arrangements in our new life.

ERNA. The man in the street envies you everything you've got, when you've worked yourself up to something and own your own business. Because you're bound to have a bit of nice jewellery, and maybe even a shiny car. Which means that a person who's worked hard can make frequent visits to Lourdes and Medjugorje, only not in a stinking bus. But it's always the same. You finally get your reward for a life spent hard at work, and people straight away start throwing filth at you. And those elements are going to keep on doing it until everything true, and everything fine, is drowned in urine and excrement.

MARIEDL (*wriggling*). Meee, it's my turn to . . .

GRETE. Oh go on. Get your filthy imaginings out of your system. Then Erna and I can start thinking about serious problems.

MARIEDL (*agitated, scratching herself all over*). The people have all left the toilet again. Everyone's gone. No-one remains behind except Mariedl. Mariedl stands there with her empty perfume bottle, because she's drunk it all, and inside she smells like all the rich ladies in the world all put together. But on the outside, she's still covered in poo, and it makes her a little bit sad. My beauty lies in my soul, she thinks to herself, but the trouble is, my soul is such a long way in. The soul is feeding on eternity, but meanwhile the only thing anyone sees is your body all your life. And she's cut herself on the tin of goulasch. And the beer's all gone, she's drunk all that as well, and Mariedl feels really sick. Because Hungarian goulasch and French perfume don't really mix well in the body. It can be very lonely in a toilet when you're all alone and you haven't got anything big or small you need to do. So poor Mariedl pulls herself together and washes off the worst of the stool. She wants to be with all the other people pursuing their happiness at the party. So she goes in there and warms herself to the merry sound of

the music. She sees Grete, hopping about and giggling
because that big blond fatso is trying to put his finger up her
dress again. She sees Erna and Wottila pledging their love
with a cup of milk coffee. And everyone's got so much joy
in their heart it's almost running over, like a blocked toilet.
But life obeys its own laws, and conjures up mortal danger
from its calm surface. Outside the party, a taxi has pulled
up, and out of it get two people, a man and a woman. They
haven't even paid the driver, and he's running after them,
shouting: Oi where's my fare. But the man just says, the old
women inside will cough up for it, so the three of them go
in. And they see a little dog tied up, a dachshund, it's called
Lydi, and the woman gives it such a terrible kick that it falls
down and doesn't get up again.

GRETE. Aaaaaah, that bitch, that whore, who is she?

ERNA *is listening with interest and signals to* GRETE *to be quiet.* GRETE *carries on sobbing quietly.*

ERNA. Go on, Mariedl.

MARIEDL (*leans back and closes her eyes*). Grete recognises
Hannelore straight away, even at a distance. (GRETE *sobs harder.*) Grete turns as white as a sheet and all she can do is
stammer: Where is Australia, anyway? Hannelore comes
straight up to Grete and without saying a word, she gives
her a couple of mighty whacks across the face, and Grete's
false teeth fall out and her wig's been knocked sideways.
Then she says to Grete that this irritating man behind her is
a taxi driver wanting to be paid and that Grete will have to
pay him, because from now on, all bills are going to have to
be paid out of Grete's meagre life savings. Grete can only
howl, and the dribble runs down from her mouth.

GRETE *yells and hurls herself at* MARIEDL. ERNA *is too fast for* GRETE *and holds her back.*

ERNA. Don't try to prevent Mariedl from looking into reality,
she may be about to see my life's happiness with Wottila.
We have to be able to endure the truth, Grete, we have to
stand on our feet staring the truth in the face, even if our
feet are swollen . . . Go on, Mariedl.

GRETE *has collapsed into her chair and is shaking.*
MARIEDL *closes her eyes again and speaks.*

MARIEDL. Freddy's quite lost his appetite for sticking his finger in Grete's bum. He's looking with embarrassment at the false teeth lying on the dirty floor. And because he finds it all so distressing, he takes his money out. The taxi driver keeps laughing stupidly all the time and he asks Freddy what sort of a necrophiliac Freddy is, and Grete's sitting there all dishevelled. Freddy puts down two banknotes on the table and says he's really been stitched up by the old bag. Then Hannelore laughs out loud and whacks Grete again a couple of times and her wig falls right off. The same people who previously were gathered around the surprise toilets are now standing around Grete as if she were a toilet that's blocked. And one of them says, look, that woman has shat herself. Freddy gets still more uncomfortable. He puts another two notes down on the table then he stands up, finishes his beer and goes over and joins the onlookers. Then someone comes in, and throws something down on the floor, and says: Whose dead dog is this?

GRETE. Lydiii. (GRETE *is having convulsions. She is clenching her fists and her face is distorted.*)

ERNA. Life brings up many a flower from hell into this vale of tears.

MARIEDL. Meanwhile people are getting restless again, because there isn't anything more for them to look at. Grete has buried herself under an old newspaper and doesn't move. Hannelore is on the telephone to the lunatic asylum. But on the far side of the room a crowd quickly gathers because Herrmann is stumbling among the tables. He's big and bloated and completely drunk.

GRETE *is sitting up again. Her make-up has run and she's very dishevelled.*

Out of my way, he shouts, I have to get to my mum and her butcher, I have to examine her, to find out if he's had the old sow. Erna sits there as if struck by lightning, and Wottila's got such a look on his face, anyone would think he'd had another vision of the Virgin Mary. Herrmann sits down with a crash and shouts: Waiter . . . a barrel of beer, to flush the communion wafers down.

ERNA *stands up making threatening gestures and moving towards* MARIEDL. GRETE *grabs* ERNA *and pushes her down in her chair again.* GRETE *holds* ERNA *there until* ERNA *hides her head in her apron.*

GRETE. You need to keep sight of the truth as well, Erna. Life consumes whatever it wants. It can bring you a hard stool one day and a soft one the next. And whatever kind of stool life brings to you, well that's providence, and there's nothing you can do about it. So be a brave girl, and wait . . . till it's over. Go on, Mariedl.

MARIEDL. Wottila is the first one to pull himself together, and he says to Herrmann: How can you presume to speak in such a way of the woman who gave you the gift of life? Herrmann stands up, wipes his shoes on Wottila's suit, then empties a cup of milk coffee over Wottila's bald head. Wottila swiftly pulls his handkerchief from his trouser pocket and starts calmly doing battle with the coffee on his jacket. Then he says: May God forgive you, Herrmann, for what you do to him every second of your life. Each drop of blood from Christ's wounds only serves to flush you ever deeper into hell. And Herrmann says: What do you say to that, mum, what do you think about the way this exploiter of dead animals is speaking to your son? But Erna just squawks like a half-strangled goose. She probably isn't getting enough air, because it's so stuffy with all the spectators crowding round. But she still has just enough strength to spit in Herrmann's face. But Herrmann just falls about laughing. One pig spitting in another pig's face, he says, what difference does that make to anything. Then he calmly stands up, smooths back his hair, grabs Erna and Wottila by the scruffs of their necks, and bashes their heads together till the blood comes pouring out and their souls depart from this world. (*She breathes in deeply and stretches.*) And what of Mariedl standing there?

Mariedl stands there triumphant over all worldly things, with rays streaming out between her legs. And the people's stool on her is all turning into gold dust. Meanwhile everyone's attacked Herrmann and tied him up and they keep on beating the scriptures into him with their fists till the police arrive. But Mariedl is floating up above the people, and everyone goes quiet, because they can see Mariedl's skin peeling off under the weight of the gold dust. She floats across to Erna and Wottila, who will be buried together, and strews a little bit of gold dust on their poor battered heads. Then the beautiful Mariedl floats over to poor Herrmann, who's never going to be let out of prison again, and bequeaths some gold dust to him as well. And Grete has to have some, because she's going straight to the loony bin, Hannelore has already fixed that up. And before Lore goes back to Australia, she too receives a sprinkle of gold from Mariedl.

Meanwhile ERNA *and* GRETE *have stood up, and are inspecting the kitchen knives on* ERNA's *sideboard.* ERNA *exits quietly to fetch a rag and bucket.*

Mariedl's feet no longer know any pain, the floating is doing her good, also her feet are getting smaller and life is getting bigger and bigger. Even the priest doesn't look any bigger than a blowfly, because he's so far away. Up and up she floats. Lourdes is down there, it's the size of a matchbox. And there goes the Virgin Mary flying along, she has to go and appear to someone . . . she's hardly any bigger than a beetle. She looks very kind, the poor little thing.

Determinedly and very pragmatically, ERNA *and* GRETE *approach* MARIEDL. *They carefully cut her throat all the way across.* ERNA *is ready with bucket and rag to prevent any excessive mess.*

ERNA. Isn't it strange how a person smells from the inside.
And why do people have so much blood in their flesh?
I wouldn't be surprised if this one had a turd in her head as well. I'd really be interested to know.

GRETE. The tongue looks all right, I'll take that home for Lydi.

ERNA. Bright red blood, isn't it peaceful . . . you'd think everything would be going wild in someone who's just died.

GRETE. What shall we do with it?

ERNA. We'll bury her in the cellar, because everyone's got a body buried in their cellar, that's what they're always saying about this country.

End of Scene Two.

Scene Three

The stage is a theatre. A small, grubby auditorium; a tiny stage framed in lightbulbs. The 'audience' sit on benches, backs to the real audience. During the performance, waitresses serve beer. The Original Breech-Loading Soul Soothers are on stage. The 'audience' shouts and yells.

LEAD SINGER. And before the play, one last great song from the Original Breech-Loading Soul Soothers, this one's entitled 'What I'd like the Lord to be for me'.

Shouts and yells from the AUDIENCE.

If Jesus were an omnibus
I know He'd get me there
I'd climb up on that omnibus
And then I'd say my prayers

If Jesus were an omelette
How much He'd cost to make
You'd need a thousand eggs at least
And in your heart they'd break

If Jesus were a milk machine
The world would be His cow
Your heart is full of precious milk
And Jesus needs it now

If Jesus were an apple tree
His apples would be green
The sweet ones would be out of reach
And few and far between

If Jesus were a typewriter
You'd be the smallest key
So don't forget to taptaptap
Until your soul is free

Yes Jesus is the House of God
And you must be the heat
Be sure to keep your heart switched on
So you can warm His feet

Yes Jesus is a launderette
He'll wash you till you're clean
He'll wash away the dirty spots
Put your soul in His machine

A pressure cooker Jesus is
To cook you till you're soft
He'll cook your head until it's light
And send your soul aloft

There's a noisy farewell to the Original Breech-Loading Soul Soothers. The curtain falls then rises again. Three pretty young women are acting on the little stage, performing HOLY MOTHERS *viciously, stridently, and with exaggeration. The 'audience' laughs, and applauds at various points.*

ERNA, GRETE *and* MARIEDL, *sitting among the 'audience', soon stand up horrified and try to leave. This is difficult because they are seated in the middle of a row.* ERNA *is the first to succeed in escaping and rattles one of the exit doors, which is closed.* GRETE *can't find an open door either. Only* MARIEDL *finds one. She rushes over to* GRETE *and drags her to the open door.* GRETE *frees herself, rushes to* ERNA *and drags her to the open door as well. All three disappear.* HOLY MOTHERS *continues on the stage for a while.*

End.

PARROTS' LIES

(*Die Lügen der Papageien*)

by Andreas Marber

translated by David Tushingham

Andreas Marber was born in Southwest Germany in 1961 and has worked as a dramaturg in various theatres since 1985. He has been chief dramaturg at the Schauspielhaus Bochem from 1996 to 1999. His plays include: *Die Nazisirene* (1990), *Das Sind Sie Schon Gewesen Die Besseren Tage* (1994), *Die Lügen der Papageien* (1995), *Rimbaud in Eisenhüttenstadt* (1997), *Die Freuden Liegen Unverbraucht und Wenig Vesucht Vor Uns* (2000) and a play for radio, *Frau Anna B. Kommt in den Vierten Stock.*

Parrots' Lies was first performed in English as a rehearsed reading in the *New German Voices* season in the Theatre Upstairs on 5 October 1997 with the following cast:

THE AUTHOR	Terry Johnson
THE DIRECTOR	Phyllida Lloyd
THE ACTOR	Darren Tighe
THE SOUND OPERATOR	Fergus O'Hare
THE STAGE MANAGER	Pea Horsley

Director Fiona Shaw
Translator David Tushingham

Characters

THE ACTOR (*male*)
THE DIRECTOR (*female*)
THE AUTHOR (*male*)

The events and characters are fictional. In performance the names of The Actor, The Director and The Author should be replaced with the performers' own names. The names of the offstage characters may also be replaced with others more appropriate to the situation of that particular performance.

The play is set in the present in a rehearsal room.

Darkness.

THE DIRECTOR.
　Tell me when you're ready.

THE ACTOR.
　Right.

THE DIRECTOR.
　Ok
　And – lights.

The lights come on. On stage THE ACTOR *lies curled up in a ball. Pause.*

THE ACTOR.
　I'm a piece of –

He's struggling to find the right expression.

　Shit I can't do it.

THE DIRECTOR.
　Well have another go
　Can we have the lights down again
　And Pea let's try bringing them up
　A bit slower this time
　It'll give him more time.

Lights off.

THE DIRECTOR.
　Thanks
　Are we ready.

THE ACTOR.
　Yes.

THE DIRECTOR.
　Ok then quiet everyone please and – lights.

The stage is lit, albeit more slowly than before.

THE ACTOR.
> I'm a piece of shit.

> *Pause.*

THE ACTOR.
> I'm a piece of shit.

> *Pause.*

THE ACTOR.
> No hang on
> I've almost got it
> I'm a piece of shit
> No
> I'm – a –
> Fuck

THE DIRECTOR.
> Look there's no point in
> Getting too hung up
> On this bit now
> Perhaps we should take another look
> At something else.

THE ACTOR.
> No I want
> To get through this today
> Let me have another go
> Without the lights
> Once I've cracked this bit
> I reckon that's the whole play sorted.

THE DIRECTOR.
> Though that was rather good
> Just now
> I think the light
> Slowly fading in like that helps.

THE ACTOR.
> I know but again
> That's just technical
> I feel there's
> A more fundamental problem
> With this line.

THE DIRECTOR.
>   But you know how important it is in the play
>   That line
>   Is where the title comes from
>   And the name
>   Of the lead character
>   It has to be there
>   For the play as a whole.

THE ACTOR.
>   'Course.

In a different tone.

>   I just don't see
>   Why the play has to be called
>   'A Piece of Shit'
>   Which means the title role has to be
>   'A Piece of Shit'
>   And he then has to go and say that too –
>   I mean I can sort of understand
>   But my feelings about it
>   Are something else entirely.

THE DIRECTOR.
>   I think we should talk about this later
>   Right now let's just get on and do it.

THE ACTOR.
>   Alright
>   I just don't want us
>   To look for another purely technical solution.

THE DIRECTOR.
>   I don't know
>   What you mean by 'another purely technical solution'
>   I thought
>   The lights might help that's all
>   We don't have to do it like that.

THE ACTOR.
>   I need to know
>   What that line's doing there
>   Then I can play it no problem.

THE DIRECTOR.
Maybe one way to approach it
Is
That the character could be wrong
That he might not genuinely believe
What he says
Or he's simply repeating
Somebody else's words
Picking up on
Someone else's view of themselves
The way I see it this line –
To a certain extent it's about our situation
When what we do stops being theatre
And starts to become something very different
When that line comes out
People have really got to believe you
You can't just somehow
Act it
I think
With this character
In this play
At this moment
You've got to absolutely
Be it
One hundred per cent
But we don't want to
Talk the play to death.

THE ACTOR.
Yeah I know.

Pause. He lies down on the floor, again curled up though differently from before.

THE ACTOR.
Maybe it's more like
A piece of shit
I'm a piece of shit
How's that.

THE DIRECTOR.
You're on the right track
So shall we try that again

>   Hold on I'll just
>   Quickly sort out
>   The lights
>   I'll just be a minute
>   Pea can we have some lights please
>   Not the whole thing
>   Just a rehearsal state.

VOICE. Ok.

THE DIRECTOR.
>   I'll give you your cue
>   Darren are you all set.

THE ACTOR.
>   Yes.

THE DIRECTOR.
>   And – cue.

THE ACTOR.
>   I'm –
>
>   *He weeps.*
>
>   I can't do it
>   I just can't do it today.

THE DIRECTOR.
>   Look it's not
>   As bad as all that.

THE ACTOR.
>   I keep on getting the feeling
>   I'm missing something in this scene
>   The scene needs something more.

THE DIRECTOR.
>   Like what.

THE ACTOR.
>   I don't know.

THE DIRECTOR.
>   What sort of thing are you thinking of
>   Do you mean props
>   I don't think though this scene's going to work
>   Because of a prop
>   Or music or whatever.

THE ACTOR.
> Music though
> I think that's
> An excellent idea
> Music
> Something far eastern.

THE DIRECTOR.
> I don't think so.

THE ACTOR.
> But we could give it a try.

THE DIRECTOR.
> Yes we could
> But I don't think
> It's going to work.

THE ACTOR.
> Let's try it.

THE DIRECTOR.
> I just think
> The focus of this scene lies elsewhere
> I think the quality
> Of this moment is
> That at this point in the play
> When we already know
> Such a lot about the character
> The play is named after
> All you do is lie there
> And say
> I'm a piece of shit
> And because the play's called
> A Piece of Shit
> Suddenly theatrical truth
> And reality
> Overlap
> And everyone in the audience will see
> You're not just acting
> For you it's true
> You really are a piece of shit
> In that moment
> As far as you and everyone else is concerned.

THE ACTOR.
　Yeah I understand all that
　You've explained it so many times
　But I still can't get it
　I don't know –
　Claire
　I'm a bit scared
　That you can't give me
　What I need
　For this part
　But
　Perhaps
　I really would like to try it with the music
　Just once.

THE DIRECTOR.
　Look I can get you music
　That's not the problem
　I just don't believe
　That music is what this moment is about.

　A knock.

THE ACTOR.
　Shit.

THE DIRECTOR.
　This is a rehearsal
　Fuck's sake.

　THE AUTHOR *enters the room.*

THE AUTHOR.
　I know.

THE DIRECTOR.
　Oh it's you.

THE AUTHOR.
　I just wanted to see how it's going.

THE DIRECTOR.
　It's going fine.

THE AUTHOR.
　I was feeling a bit bored
　And of course I'm curious
　You don't mind if I –

THE DIRECTOR.
> Now's not really the best time
> It's really not
>
> *To* THE ACTOR.
>
> Is it.

THE AUTHOR.
> I saw the call sheet
> Today you're doing the scene
> Where he has to stand alone and . . .
> I'd like to watch.

THE DIRECTOR.
> No look
> We've reached a point in the process now
> Where that really isn't a good idea.

THE AUTHOR.
> You're always at that point in the process
> It's not on
> That I don't get to see the play
> Before the opening.

THE DIRECTOR.
> But it's not on today either.

THE AUTHOR.
> I don't like this.

THE DIRECTOR.
> I don't care.

THE AUTHOR.
> I want to see the scene now.

THE DIRECTOR.
> But we don't want you to.

THE AUTHOR.
> Alright.
> If I don't
> See the scene now
> Someone else
> Can direct the play
> That's what I agreed with

Malcolm
I'm not going to be fucked around like this
It's my play
And I can look at it when
I
Want and not when you've decided you're
Ready.

THE DIRECTOR.
Did you really agree that with Malcolm.

THE AUTHOR.
I don't understand
What's so bad about that
It's not as if
I'm your enemy.

THE ACTOR.
What do you mean
Then you can get someone else to direct the play.

THE AUTHOR.
I agreed with Malcolm
That if I don't see the scene today
Either it'll be done
By a new director
With a new leading actor
Or it's cancelled.

THE ACTOR.
Fuck you.

THE DIRECTOR.
Darren.

THE ACTOR *exits*.

THE DIRECTOR.
There was no need to go and do that.

THE AUTHOR.
Do you want to get him now or are you going to
Wait a while
Listen
I've had enough pissing about
An author's rights in his own play

>Are what they fought
>The French Revolution for
>One of the things
>And I'm not letting you
>Take them away from me.

THE DIRECTOR.
>That's bollocks
>That's not what this is about at all
>And you know it

>*Pause.*

>You're punishing Darren for something else altogether.

THE AUTHOR.
>There might be something in that

>*Pause.*

>Considering he's got two kids
>And he hardly works
>He's staying out there a long time.

THE DIRECTOR.
>That's really mean
>And you know it is.

THE AUTHOR.
>Then it's mean
>Of you not to understand
>What does it matter
>If I'm there
>I don't want to
>Pass judgement on it
>I only want to be able to see it
>Then I'll go away again
>I'll not say a word
>If that's what you want
>But you've got to understand
>That it's important
>To me
>And perhaps
>I can be some help
>Look

We've known each other so long now
Done so many shows together
And here you are directing my play
That should mean something shouldn't it
To both of us.

THE DIRECTOR.
I think the play's
Terrific
I wouldn't be doing it if I didn't
But I don't understand
Why you've got to abuse the power it gives you
Over the two of us
Darren and me.

THE AUTHOR.
I think
You two are abusing yours
When you say
I can't be there
That's Darren's
Petty revenge
Against me.

THE DIRECTOR.
And what I want –

THE ACTOR *returns*. THE AUTHOR *goes to one side*. THE ACTOR *looks at* THE DIRECTOR.

THE DIRECTOR.
Darren
Sorry
I was slightly caught on the hop there
But I just feel now
We have reached a stage in the process
Where we have got something to show
I think it might be rather good
To have Patrick here
He might be able to tell us something
Useful.

THE ACTOR.
I don't
Mind.

THE AUTHOR *sits down.*

THE DIRECTOR (*to* THE AUTHOR).
The way we've staged it is that
Just before –
You need to
Imagine it with the music
And the lights
Where he is now
There's a spot
That makes his hands and face look
Completely white
Of course we're
Not all the way there yet
We were in the middle of
Darren was just trying
To find a way in to the text
So much of this play is
About an actor identifying
With his character.

THE AUTHOR.
Of course.

THE DIRECTOR.
Ready.

THE ACTOR.
Yes.

THE DIRECTOR.
I'll give you the cue
And Darren remember
What we said about
Explore
Till you're more or less there
Then we'll see
Right
Then – lights.

THE ACTOR.
I'm a piece of shit
I'm a piece of shit
I'm a piece of shit.

THE AUTHOR *holds his hand in front of his mouth and laughs. As* THE ACTOR *repeats his line with growing desperation, waves of laughter shake* THE AUTHOR*'s body, which to begin with he can control quite well.* THE DIRECTOR *notices. Suddenly* THE AUTHOR *snorts loudly and slaps his thigh.*

THE AUTHOR.
 He's saying it
 He's actually saying it.

THE DIRECTOR.
 What is it.

THE AUTHOR.
 He's actually saying it.

THE ACTOR *does not notice anything. Meanwhile* THE AUTHOR *is giggling so much, he has to lie down on the floor and hold his stomach.*

THE AUTHOR.
 I don't believe it
 He's actually saying it.

THE ACTOR.
 I'm a piece of shit.

THE AUTHOR.
 He's saying that for money
 That is un-fucking-believable
 No-one's going to believe this.

THE ACTOR *sees him. He stands up and looks at* THE AUTHOR, *who is still pulsating with laughter.* THE ACTOR*'s eyes water. Snorting with rage, literally, he walks out of the rehearsal room and slams the door as hard as he can.*

THE DIRECTOR.
 Darren.

THE DIRECTOR *follows* THE ACTOR. *In the doorway she turns round to the laughing Author.*

THE DIRECTOR.
 You're such a cunt.

Exit THE DIRECTOR.

THE AUTHOR (*slapping his thigh*).
He said it
He actually said it
He stood up on stage and said
He's a piece of shit
That's priceless
If anyone had told me that
I mean I'd shoot myself
Before getting up on stage and saying –
I may be
The biggest jerk in the world
But I'm not going to stand up
On stage and say so not like that
Not so everyone believes it's true.

THE DIRECTOR *returns.*

THE DIRECTOR.
Darren's completely lost it.

THE AUTHOR.
He'll recover.

THE DIRECTOR.
Was that strictly necessary.

THE AUTHOR.
I hadn't planned
It was just the sight of him lying there
I never imagined it would be
Quite so gobsmacking.

THE DIRECTOR.
What did you have to go and do that for
I've spent weeks trying
To explain to Darren
That the part
Has nothing to do with him.

THE AUTHOR.
But why
He's perfect casting.

THE DIRECTOR.
Darren won't play it

If he feels someone's
Taking the piss.

THE AUTHOR.
Darren's going to play it alright
It's the only title role
Darren'll ever play in his life
The title role in
A Piece of Shit
If he plays this one
Perhaps he'll get others
But if he doesn't
He'll be doing bit parts for the rest of his life
If that
Let's face it
That was some acting he was doing there –

THE DIRECTOR.
You hardly saw any of it.

THE AUTHOR.
But you're not telling me
What I saw
Even had flashes of being
Tolerable
The way he was lying there
It would have brought a tear to the eye
Of every physiotherapist in the country.

THE DIRECTOR.
He's never played the scene
That badly before
It might have had something to do with
You being here.

THE AUTHOR.
Bollocks
I mean if he'd ever learnt how to speak properly
He wouldn't have to play parts like that
But now it's all my fault
People have either got it or they haven't.

THE DIRECTOR.
That's not right though

There's another thing
You're always giving off signals
To people you can't stand
It's like you're saying
'Go on I know
You're going to fail anyway'
And it affects those people to such an extent
That they completely screw up
Just to prove you right
Because they can tell you expect
Them to fail
And they don't want to
Disappoint you
So they fail
As a way of respecting your opinion.

THE AUTHOR.
I'll have to work on that.

THE DIRECTOR.
It's what happens
And another thing do you realise
How hard you're making it for me
To convince Darren
The part isn't
About humiliating him
It's about –

THE AUTHOR.
But that's exactly what it is about.

THE DIRECTOR.
You fuckwit
We've all been telling him
It's something more than that
It's a good play
If he finds out.

THE AUTHOR.
He already knows
Life's tough
This is Darren's big break
Title role

A piece of shit in a play that's called
A Piece of Shit
That's like Hamlet in Hamlet
No-one's ever going to cast Darren as Hamlet
But a piece of shit
That's something Darren can aspire to.

THE DIRECTOR.
He's not aspiring to anything
He's sitting outside crying.

THE AUTHOR.
Well it's a start
Considering he's c/o Spotlight
He's crying an awfully long time.

THE DIRECTOR.
You are so evil
Now you've even got me hoping
This play backfires on you.

THE AUTHOR.
How is that going to happen
If the play gets on
Darren'll stand on stage and say
'I'm a piece of shit'
That's all I want
And if it doesn't get performed
Then Darren'll hang around the bar
Saying he refused
To play the lead
In some shit play of mine
And no-one will listen
It's just one of a whole load of plays
He won't be playing the lead in.

THE DIRECTOR.
You know I thought
This play was about something else
You told me
It was about the position we're all in
About
How we can make

What's said on stage
Be taken seriously again
And in a broader sense
To restore some kind of relevance
To the theatre
By examining the way
Actors identify with their parts.

THE AUTHOR.
Of course I said that
But I didn't seriously expect
You to believe it
All I want to do
Is get my own back on Darren.

THE DIRECTOR.
But why pick on Darren.

THE AUTHOR.
Look I respect Darren
By taking him so seriously.

THE DIRECTOR.
You do realise
The entire company
Think this exercise stinks
And that's being polite
Even the ones who can't stand Darren
Think the play is unnecessary
And cruel.

THE AUTHOR.
Yes I do realise that
But you know what the great thing about it is
No-one's said anything about it to me
Because they all know
If they go mouthing off at me
Or anyone I know
Dishing any kind of dirt about me
It goes straight in the play
Since I wrote this play
People don't bother me
With any of this crap any more

I've got time to think
About important things
If all this play achieves
Is that I spend two months not being pestered by morons
Purely out of fear
Then it'll have been worth it
If you knew some of the stuff
I've had to listen to
Enough.

THE DIRECTOR.
What I really can't understand
Is why you picked out Darren
I mean he's such an easy target
Because he's got no means of defending himself
Now he's sitting out there
Feeling he's made a total prat of himself
A complete arsehole.

THE AUTHOR.
Well that's what he is
This play will help Darren come to terms with himself
In a playful way
Just as it will also help others to recognize
What a tosser Darren is
A lot of people didn't even know who Darren was
Until I wrote this play
I'm not getting my own back on Darren
I'm offering him a part
If he doesn't play it he won't play anything
All he has to do is play himself.

THE DIRECTOR.
Darren isn't playing himself in the part.

THE AUTHOR.
Oh yes he is, that's exactly what he's doing.

THE DIRECTOR.
But the part isn't called Darren
It's called 'A Piece of Shit'.

THE AUTHOR.
Right
And because Darren is a piece of shit –

THE DIRECTOR.
  I don't find that at all funny

THE AUTHOR.
  I do
  A lot
  I think it's funny
  Making bitchy jokes about other people
  I just can't laugh
  When someone makes one about me

  Pause.

  To be honest
  I was wondering
  Whether it ought to have a different title
  For other reasons
  If the posters all say
  A Piece of Shit
  No-one's going to come
  Doesn't matter who's in it
  You could have Ewan MacGregor in it
  Still nobody'll come
  I'd prefer a
  Hmm
  More attractive
  Title
  Something harmless.

THE DIRECTOR.
  Have you got one.

THE AUTHOR.
  I once did
  A play about actors
  And the problem they've got
  Only ever saying other people's words
  It was about
  Whether parrots are ever afraid
  Of someone saying something in front of them
  They have to repeat
  Without understanding
  And if they do understand it

They have to repeat it
Against their will
This fear
Parrots have
Of repeating an obscene word
Because they can't stop themselves
Is the same as an actor's fear
Of bad writing
Panicky parrots
Parrots' panic
Sounds quite good.

THE DIRECTOR.
You'd be doing yourself a favour
I can tell you
And me and Darren and rest of the theatre.

THE AUTHOR.
Course Darren
Would no longer have the title role.

THE DIRECTOR.
I don't think
He'd mind –

In a different tone.

Are you serious
Do you think you've understood
Anything about the theatre
Or have you not got a clue
About acting

Pause.

Do you hate the theatre.

THE AUTHOR.
I love the theatre
I love you
I love Darren
I want Darren to have a title role
And the only play
With Darren in the title role
Has to be a Piece of Shit
Shame about the parrots.

THE DIRECTOR.
>But why
>What did he ever do to you.

THE AUTHOR.
>You know what.

THE DIRECTOR.
>Yes I do know.

THE AUTHOR.
>He was in the lunch queue with Mark Evans and said –

THE DIRECTOR.
>I know.

THE AUTHOR.
>That a group of them should go and see Malcolm
>On behalf of the company
>And tell him
>My plays are unperformable.

THE DIRECTOR.
>I know
>He says
>He said nothing of the kind.

THE AUTHOR.
>And that I ought to jack it in
>He couldn't go on
>With this pretentious drivel any longer.

THE DIRECTOR.
>I know
>But loads of people say that about you.

THE AUTHOR.
>I don't care
>Only Darren's mistake was
>I found out
>I don't mind
>What anyone says behind my back
>Lisa says she stuck up for me
>And said I'd done some stuff
>That was alright
>It's incredible

I think it was really sweet of Lisa
To support me the way she did
And to tell me about it
I mean my jaw just dropped
When I heard that
He must have a screw loose
Malcolm tried to reassure me
You always try to act like it doesn't bother you
But this was the last straw.

THE DIRECTOR.
Darren can't help that though.

THE AUTHOR.
No
No more or less than any of the others
Darren went and opened his gob
When he should have kept it shut
What really makes you sick about this job
Is every moron
Yeah really every single moron
Can come along and pour a bucket of shit over you
In the whole of London there are four people
Five maybe
Who can tell the difference between a good scene and a bad one
Apart from Malcolm and myself I don't know who they are
But there must be some somewhere
Purely statistically
There are more than eight million people living here.

THE DIRECTOR.
Now don't get upset
And stop shouting at me
I don't think
Malcolm would agree
With what you've just been saying.

THE AUTHOR (*shouts*).
And everyone else should shut the fuck up
But instead of that an actor
Whose face would explode
If he ever tried saying

A single decent sentence
Thinks he's got to express a verdict on my plays
If this play here
Makes any sense at all
Then it's to keep
All this crap
Away from me
To stop them
Telling me what they think
Showering me with whatever shit fills their brains
This play is my public statement
That I do not want to be criticised
By anybody
I've got enough trouble handling my self-criticism
But at least I can read
Whereas these illiterates
Should belt up
I don't care
They can say what they want
As long as it's in secret and out of my hearing
Never mind if it seems arrogant or stupid
They can find someone else
Next time they –

THE DIRECTOR.
Oh come off it please
None of that's any use now
If you wanted to say that
You should have put it in the fucking play.

THE AUTHOR.
You want me
To make a prat of myself
But I want to make a prat out of Darren
And if anyone no matter who
Starts talking crap about me in public
Then I'll make a prat of them too
D'you understand
I'll wipe them off the face of the planet
I'm going to write a play
About every person

Who has ever come up to me and said something stupid
Don't feed the fucking author
It bites.

THE DIRECTOR.
You never did want to see
The fucking rehearsal
You just wanted to vent your little spleen.

THE AUTHOR.
Really.

THE DIRECTOR.
Patrick the least you could do
Is give us different names in the play.

THE AUTHOR.
I thought about that
There is something to be said for it.

THE DIRECTOR.
It would be the same play
It just wouldn't be quite so
Destructive.

THE AUTHOR.
You've been talking to Sarah.

THE DIRECTOR.
Why did you have to use our names.

THE AUTHOR.
I can tell you that
Names are arbitrary
And coincidental
Just as arbitrary
And coincidental
As any other names might be
Which means it's quite arbitrary
And coincidental
That they happen to be our own
It's hard making up names
And there might be some good reasons
For doing it
But if you look at them all these reasons are

Moral ethical politically correct
They're not
Artistic
Any play which alters the names of its characters
Purely out of ethical considerations
Is no more than
Masturbation
In a rather expensive and time-consuming form
I can't be bothered
To talk about say Dominic Fear
Without using his name
But in a way that everyone recognizes
Dominic Fear's who I mean
Or Brian Steen
Putting it into some sort of code
Would be stupid
It's just too much work
For me
And the audience
And it's not worth it
Theatre's got to be spontaneous
You need to be able to understand it
Without all sorts of background knowledge
You really shouldn't be asking me
What I've got against Darren
I've done something for him
I've written this play for him
The best thing would be
When he still didn't know about it
When he'd see me and say hello
And I'd say hello too
Knowing that he was supposed to say
I'm a piece of shit
And he didn't know
That was brilliant
He was staying with Craig
In the flat downstairs
And I'd see the two of them chatting
Maybe he told him
I ought to jack it in

And I was out on the balcony
Typing away tap tap tap
Little did he know
I was swinging the
Cudgel that's now going to come
Splat
Right down on top of him.

THE DIRECTOR.
Sometimes I ask myself
Why do I have to know somebody like you
What did I do
You're so petty and so vindictive
Over nothing
He just let it slip out
You could be a little bit more generous
And overlook the whole thing
Find something important
Write a play about that
And stop wasting your time and everyone else's
With this great big schoolboy joke.

THE AUTHOR.
I'd be careful there if I were you
Not even Malcolm said
This is a schoolboy joke
But you can go up to his office
And tell him what you think
He's occasionally there.

THE DIRECTOR.
Anyway all that stuff with the names is irrelevant
I mean in the play
There's a female director who happens to be called
Claire and I'm called
Claire but that doesn't make me identify with her
At all.

THE AUTHOR.
Do you identify Darren with his part.

THE DIRECTOR.
A little bit.

THE AUTHOR.
See and Darren does the same with you.

THE DIRECTOR.
If I'd
Really said the things I say in here
I'd throw myself under a bus.

THE AUTHOR.
That would be worth writing a play about
Lorna keeps saying
I really ought to write
A three-hander
I mean I think three-handers are
Boring
'My friend Serge bought a painting'
Except this one
I think
It's fun
Now go and find your leading man.

THE DIRECTOR.
You little sod.

THE AUTHOR.
You see this is a game
I can't lose
Either the play goes on
In which case the fact that I'm a little sod
Will be obscured
By Darren standing up every night
In front of a hundred paying customers and saying
He's a piece of shit.

THE DIRECTOR.
I do not want to hear that line any more.

THE AUTHOR.
You've still got the tech to get through
Or if the play doesn't get on
Then it will share the fate of my other plays
Neither I nor anyone else will pay it much attention
And it won't matter
I don't think

Darren can get his own back
He'd have to think of something pretty spectacular.

THE DIRECTOR.
But why is Darren the one
Why does he have to suffer.

THE AUTHOR.
If he'd treated me decently
And respected me like I respected him
He wouldn't have to.

THE DIRECTOR.
You respected him did you.

THE AUTHOR.
Yes I did
It would never have occurred to me
To tell the whole lunch queue
That he's a mediocre actor
With a quarter page in Spotlight
The idea would never have entered my head
And I can't understand why he did it
I mean
My plays have had all kinds of things done to them
But I would never so much as dream
Of saying in front of everyone
That so and so really ought to find a day job
It's outrageous.

THE DIRECTOR.
Look to a certain extent I can
Sympathize with you
Why though did you have to pick on Darren
If you need an enemy
Why go for the weakest.

THE AUTHOR.
I'll tell you
Because I don't want
To get into a bad position
With anyone whose opinion actually counts for something
The funny thing is that the people
Whose opinions do count

Don't go round talking crap about me
Or if they do
They manage to do it without me noticing
I think that's good
I don't want to know about it
That's what I told Lisa
I can't write a play
Every time some little twerp comes along
And pisses on me
I'd be worn out
This took three days of my life
And all that time an unsuspecting Darren
Was wondering whether or not to go and see Malcolm
He didn't in the end
It's a shame
He should have done it
It would have been a laugh
I bet that's just what he's waiting for
Darren and Mark Evans
Giving him tips
All the things they think he could do better
I hope I can watch
It should be more than a laugh
It ought to be completely hilarious.

THE DIRECTOR.
I understand what you're saying
But you know
I really don't know
Where I fit in to all this
I've
Got thoughts about the play too
And I can't see any room for them.

THE AUTHOR.
Oh
Don't you start
Moaning.

THE DIRECTOR.
I'm not getting at you
I'm just saying –

> I'm like piggy in the middle here
> You treat me like some insignificant bimbo
> Piggy in the middle
> I can't do anything
> Because I'm stuck between the two of you
> And you both –
> I don't know where I am.

THE AUTHOR.
> Don't push it now
> You ought to be grateful –

He cuts himself off.

THE DIRECTOR.
> Grateful about what.

Pause.

THE AUTHOR.
> Nothing.

THE DIRECTOR.
> What is it
> I ought to be grateful about.

THE AUTHOR.
> Keep your hair on.

THE DIRECTOR.
> You mean I should be grateful
> I can be here at all
> Is that it.

THE AUTHOR.
> Well it's true
> We could have got a man.

THE DIRECTOR.
> You –

> THE ACTOR *enters.*

THE AUTHOR.
> Hi Darren.

THE DIRECTOR.
> Hi how are you feeling.

THE AUTHOR.
>   We were just talking about you
>   I was telling Claire
>   I think
>   You're definitely getting there
>   I'm sure it's all going to come together on the night.

THE ACTOR.
>   Yeah.

THE AUTHOR.
>   Obviously it's a tough part
>   This scene especially
>   But I think you're going about it
>   The right way
>   You're really getting right into the part
>   I'm very impressed
>   And I really don't understand
>   What everyone else's problem is
>   I
>   Think you're a bloody good actor.
>
>   THE DIRECTOR *exits outraged.*

THE ACTOR.
>   What's the matter
>   Have you been arguing.

THE AUTHOR.
>   No no she'll be back in a minute.

THE ACTOR.
>   Didn't look like that to me.

THE AUTHOR.
>   She's Welsh
>   Don't take any notice.

THE ACTOR.
>   I really like her.

THE AUTHOR.
>   Yes I know
>   Me too
>   But let's not get carried away
>   How are you getting on with it.

THE ACTOR.
    Oh it's fine
    It's a tricky scene
    The writing's tricky as well
    It's so short
    I don't know if Claire's told you
    We were wondering about a tiny rewrite here.

THE AUTHOR.
    No tell away.

THE ACTOR.
    Well instead –
    Maybe what I'm about to say is stupid
    I thought you'd already discussed this.

THE AUTHOR.
    No tell me.

THE ACTOR.
    I felt
    Where it goes
    I'm a piece of shit
    It's a little too short
    We were wondering
    If we might be able to change it slightly
    Just maybe do it more
    Now the thing is
    Perhaps I shouldn't be telling you this
    When she's not here.

THE AUTHOR.
    Just say it.

THE ACTOR.
    What we've done is
    Maybe
    Now I'd really like to say it three times in a row.

THE AUTHOR.
    Like you did before.

THE ACTOR.
    Yes like before.

THE AUTHOR.
> I liked that
> It didn't bother me at all
> You saying it three times
> Quite the opposite
> This is a performer's piece
> If anything you can experiment
> With the text even further.

THE ACTOR.
> It's a relief
> To hear you say that actually.

THE AUTHOR.
> I thought what you did there
> Was very convincing
> I think it's going to turn out rather well
> Honestly
> I think I've always slightly underestimated you
> As an actor
> I don't know why
> Lisa's a big fan of yours
> But you'd never really caught my eye
> However I think this part is going to give you
> An entirely different status in the building.

THE ACTOR.
> Patrick I've been meaning to say this for ages
> I heard
> That someone had told you
> I'd said your plays
> Were just paper
> And that you'd got quite
> Understandably quite
> Upset about that
> That's not in the slightest bit true.

THE AUTHOR.
> Look even if you had I'd have known
> You didn't mean it like that.

THE ACTOR.
> I never said it
> I'm not qualified to judge your plays.

THE AUTHOR.
> I don't have a problem with that.

THE ACTOR.
> Really
> We were talking
> Lisa was there too
> It was more of a general thing
> That we ought to go and see Malcolm
> And talk to him about all the plays.

THE AUTHOR.
> I know
> Maybe you ought to do that actually
> See Malcolm
> All go up to his office together
> And tell him what you think of the whole season.

THE ACTOR.
> But what Lisa said
> That I'd said
> That's not true.

THE AUTHOR.
> I didn't
> Believe what Lisa said
> As far as I'm concerned the whole thing's over.

THE ACTOR.
> I only wanted you to know
> That I would never
> Say anything like that.

> THE DIRECTOR *enters carrying a tray with coffee cups on it.*

THE AUTHOR.
> Oh great
> Claire's got the coffees in.

THE ACTOR.
> Wonderful.

> THE DIRECTOR *puts the tray down.*

THE DIRECTOR.
> Milk and sugar.

THE AUTHOR.
>I was just saying to Darren
>I think
>We've got a hit on our hands
>Not with the critics of course
>The critics are always going to be shit.

THE DIRECTOR.
>Who cares.

THE ACTOR.
>I don't.

THE AUTHOR.
>Neither do I
>Especially when it's
>Fear.

THE ACTOR.
>Who.

THE AUTHOR.
>Dominic Fear.

THE ACTOR.
>Who's that.

THE DIRECTOR.
>The Arts Editor of the Evening Standard.

THE AUTHOR.
>The Evening Standard doesn't have an Arts Page.

THE DIRECTOR.
>Yeah
>And Fear edits it.

THE AUTHOR.
>This play is going to test his sense of humour.

THE ACTOR.
>Will he come and see it.

THE AUTHOR.
>Not personally
>But someone definitely will
>Come and tell him he's in it
>Malcolm's behind me all the way on this

The Evening Standard
Has given us such systematically terrible reviews
We don't have to rely on them any more.

THE ACTOR.
What's he like.

THE AUTHOR.
Dominic Fear.

THE DIRECTOR.
He used to be a court reporter.

THE ACTOR.
And now he's Arts Editor
That's insane.

THE AUTHOR.
Actually there aren't any arts in it
It just says Arts on the top of the page.

THE ACTOR.
It's a good job there are
Other newspapers in London.

THE AUTHOR.
Nothing serious though.

THE ACTOR.
But I thought.

THE AUTHOR.
A lot of people think that
But it's not true
Fear was a key appointment
He was put in there
To get rid
Of the Standard's arts coverage
It's not just me who's saying that
Even his friends say so
People like J – fuck
I never told you
Fear wrote a play.

THE ACTOR.
Seriously.

THE AUTHOR.
All the world's a theatre or something
It's set in a theatre
And that's what it's about
It's an investigation of why the theatre
Has nothing to say about
Kosovo Rwanda
The Northern Ireland peace process stuff like that.

THE ACTOR.
Eh.

THE AUTHOR.
Anyhow
That's the big question
Supposedly
Wrong
In any case he wrote a play and that's what it was about
Brian the brain Steen organized a rehearsed reading
And I went with Sue and Jason
It was a scream.

THE DIRECTOR.
I know you told me already.

THE AUTHOR.
We sat there in the Almeida
And listened to this absolutely unspeakable piece of
I mean how can anyone deliberately
Make such a twat of themselves
Without even being paid for it.

THE DIRECTOR.
You told me.

THE AUTHOR.
Really be so thoroughly determined
To make a total prat of themselves
For free.

Pause. He looks at THE ACTOR.

THE AUTHOR.
I mean not even getting properly paid for it
And what was really embarrassing

Laughs.

There were scenes in the play that had just been thrown in
These horrendously talentless parodies
Did I not tell you about this.

THE DIRECTOR.
Yes.

THE AUTHOR.
And one scene

He laughs.

I couldn't believe this
He explained
That this scene had found its own way into the play

He laughs.

I looked at everyone else
None of them showed any reaction
Then he said it again
That this scene
Had joined in all by itself
I was cracking up

Still laughing.

I kept picturing this scene in front of me
Inserting itself into his play

Laughing more.

I've been writing plays for ten years
And none of them have ever
Had a scene suddenly materialize of its own accord
I had to sit there and hold it
All in
I dug my finger nails
So deep into my arm
The bruises lasted for days
I wanted to laugh so much
But I thought
If you run out now
You'll not make it to the top of the stairs
You'll be stuck there

Shouting
'It's so bad'
Over and over
And Sue saying
'But Dominic Fear can write what he likes'
And me going
'But it's sooo bad'.

THE DIRECTOR.
That was in 'Women on the Verge of a Nervous Breakdown'
And you've told it before.

THE AUTHOR (*to* THE ACTOR).
Not to you though
Jesus
That was Fear
Dominic

He has calmed down. Suddenly laughs again.

Then at the end of the scene
That just walked in by itself –

THE DIRECTOR.
I know.

THE AUTHOR.
But he doesn't
At the end of this scene with legs
Steen had to say Amen
It was

He holds his stomach.

They'd rehearsed it between them
Brain saying Amen
Holier than the fucking Pope.

THE ACTOR.
Do you fancy him.

THE AUTHOR.
Who.

THE ACTOR.
Brian Steen.

THE AUTHOR.
But he's straight.

THE ACTOR.
   Are you trying to out Brian Steen.

THE AUTHOR.
   Brian Steen is straight
   That's not outing him
   Outing him would be if I said
   Brian Steen is gay
   However
   Brian Steen is straight.

THE DIRECTOR.
   Do you want to out anybody else.

THE AUTHOR.
   Darren
   As a dickhead
   Come on Darren
   It was a joke
   Surely you can take a joke.

THE DIRECTOR.
   Anyone else.

THE AUTHOR.
   Can't be bothered
   Though it would be great
   To scare one or two people
   The worst thing about the reading was actually
   The first night we had here two days later
   I'd been sitting with Fear and we talked
   About what was wrong with his play
   And why we wouldn't put it on
   Then two days later we go and do
   This piece of absolute dogshit
   I couldn't even laugh at it
   We should have been embarrassed let alone Fear
   There was no danger of me
   Running out that night in a fit of giggles
   I was more worried
   I might start to throw up
   Marc was sitting next to me
   And he was in an equally bad way

    Afterwards was the first time
    I've ever drunk to forget
    Fear's play
    That we weren't doing
    Was bad enough
    But ours
    Was ten times worse
    Other times I get pissed
    For pleasure but that night
    I did it to forget the play
    And on top of that him indoors was out
    Couldn't even have sex afterwards
    When a play's that bad
    Sex sometimes helps.

THE ACTOR.
    You don't mind
    Tearing other people's plays
    To pieces do you.

THE AUTHOR.
    Well they're other people's.

THE ACTOR.
    But you're so sensitive
    About your own.

THE AUTHOR.
    Well they're mine aren't they
    I ought to be heading off
    I had another idea for the programme
    Darren I thought
    The poster should be a portrait of you
    Really huge and in big letters
    'Darren Durkin is whatever the title of the play'
    Then on the back we can print a target
    With a dotted line round it
    And an arrow saying
    Wank here
    And that bit's an entry form
    You can cut it out
    And whoever gets nearest the
    Bullseye

    Wins a prize
    Isn't that excellent
    I told Nigel
    He thinks it's excellent too
    And we worked out
    What the prize should be
    Which is
    Ha
    You'll never guess
    Whoever gets the closest wins
    Paper hankies
    First prize is a box
    Second to tenth prizes get one each
    Excellent.

THE DIRECTOR.
    I don't think that's a good idea.

THE AUTHOR.
    I knew you wouldn't
    Because women can't play
    Then think of a better idea
    Any suggestion's valid
    Until there's a better one
    Look I'd better be off
    I think it's coming along nicely
    Really
    And I'm going to tell Malcolm that
    Malcolm admires your acting a lot
    And I think you're doing very good work
    I think
    You're really delving
    Into the heart of the role
    To me it sounded remarkably authentic
    There was nothing imposed about it
    It was
    Like it was a matter of great personal urgency
    To stand at the front of the stage and
    Surrender yourself to the audience
    And I think you've really captured something there
    Like I said to Claire

    You're investing an enormous amount
    Of you in this part
    Anyway I don't want to talk it up too much
    There's still a long way to go before we open
    There are a few things about the text I'm not happy with
    But that's not your problem
    And then – Well that's something
    We'll have to talk about upstairs –
    Maybe it wasn't
    Such a good idea after all
    Casting you in the lead.

THE DIRECTOR.
    Patrick for God's sake.

THE AUTHOR.
    We've got to be allowed some self-criticism
    Of course you're right for the part
    But maybe it's too obvious
    Perhaps it just gets too naturalistic
    Having you as the lead
    Maybe when we were casting the play
    We should have gone more against type.

THE DIRECTOR.
    Patrick.

THE AUTHOR.
    I'm just saying
    I'm trying to be as honest as I can
    The whole play's naturalistic crap
    I'm fed up with it
    It's as if I've done an enormous dump on the stage
    And Darren's left to deal with it
    Divine was famous
    For once eating dog shit
    Just to be in a film
    Anyway I'm going to go and see Malcolm
    And tell him it's looking fine
    You're on the right track
    And it'll probably be pretty good
    Apart from the casting
    But that's our problem

We shouldn't have typecast it.

THE AUTHOR *exits.*

THE ACTOR.
Fucking arsehole.
What did he say about me when I wasn't here.

THE DIRECTOR.
He thought you were good
He thought you were absolutely
Heading in the right direction.

THE ACTOR.
Really
Is that what he said
He said that to me too
I thought he'd have said something different to you
That he was lying to me
But if he said that to you too

He reflects.

I thought I was quite good.

THE DIRECTOR.
I thought
Him being here actually
Made you rather
Surface again.

THE ACTOR.
Now I didn't think so at all
I don't think he meant it like that
What he said
Tuned in with what I felt
For the first time I thought
I've really got it
The lines aren't slipping away from me
They're flowing through me
Like an impro.

THE DIRECTOR.
Well that's not the way I saw it
So what did he say to you
When I wasn't there.

THE ACTOR.
> I talked to him
> About changing the text
> He thinks it's ok
> Me
> Saying it three times in a row.

He cries, but tries to do it without anyone noticing.

> As an actor I need
> Meat in a part like that
> I always think
> Everything in his plays is
> Far too abrupt
> The actors can never
> Get their teeth into it
> I don't care what he does to me
> The lines are paper-thin
> Can't do anything with them
> I'm a piece of shit
> Typical
> It's got no life to it
> As soon as you say it it's gone.

THE DIRECTOR.
> That's why we changed it.

THE ACTOR.
> Yes I think
> Doing it three times
> It's nice
> It's got substance.

He cries. THE DIRECTOR *shouts.*

THE DIRECTOR.
> Patrick you are such a fucking cunt.

THE ACTOR.
> What's the matter
> Claire
> What's wrong.

THE DIRECTOR.
> Nothing nothing
> I'm just knackered that's all.

THE ACTOR.
> The truth is
> He wants me to play the part
> Because he thinks I'm a piece
> Of shit
> That's it.

THE DIRECTOR.
> No no.

THE ACTOR.
> Then why does he write that sort of thing.

THE DIRECTOR.
> Look I've known him for a long time
> And we're sort of
> Friends
> He's got a lot of problems
> Personal stuff
> Sometimes I think
> He thinks he's
> A piece of shit
> The I in this play
> Who's a piece of shit
> I think that's him
> He doesn't really mean it that way
> It's just he's got so many problems in himself
> That's why he writes that sort of thing.

THE ACTOR.
> I think
> We should come back tomorrow.

THE DIRECTOR.
> I don't know
> We've got
> So little rehearsal time
> I wouldn't want to –

THE ACTOR.
> I'm so shagged.

THE DIRECTOR.
> I know.

THE ACTOR.
>   You know what
>
>   *Pause.*
>
>   I'm not going to do this play.

THE DIRECTOR.
>   Darren I know how you feel
>   There are times I want to give up
>   But if we chuck it all in –
>   Nobody will be interested.

THE ACTOR.
>   Nobody's going to be interested in this play anyway
>   Do you think anyone
>   Is going to come and see a play
>   Called 'A Piece of Shit'.

THE DIRECTOR.
>   That's just a working title
>   He said
>   He was thinking about a new one.

THE ACTOR.
>   Did he
>   That would be good I think
>   What was he thinking of then.

THE DIRECTOR.
>   Something about parrots.

THE ACTOR.
>   Parrots.

THE DIRECTOR.
>   Yes because he thinks
>   When actors have to say their lines
>   Then they're afraid of
>   Well not afraid of course
>   Perhaps more uneasy about
>   What's in them
>   That's what he thinks
>   At least that's how I understood it
>   The same way parrots are afraid
>   Of repeating a word
>   They don't understand

Actors are
Chained to language like a parrot
To its perch.

THE ACTOR.
Perch.

THE DIRECTOR.
The thing it's chained to
And keeps crapping all over.

THE ACTOR.
So what does he want to call the play.

THE DIRECTOR.
Something like
Parrots' panic or anxiety or whatever.

THE ACTOR.
Sounds a hell of a lot better
Than
A Piece of Shit

Pause.

You can tell him
That might be right
About actors saying their lines
But when some little turd like him
Just copies other plays
Really badly
Then it's embarrassing
More than embarrassing.

THE DIRECTOR.
Don't say embarrassing
It's what he always says.

THE ACTOR.
Still I'd prefer it
If the play had some other title.

THE DIRECTOR.
Yes but then you wouldn't have
The title role any more
Maybe you should tell him
You don't mind.

THE ACTOR.
Right I will
You know what
Maybe then the part'll be called
A Parrot
Because if a parrot said it
Then I'd understand what he was trying to do with the play
That'd explain the whole conflict
Let's give it another go
This scene we're on now
Is the hardest
We need an idea like we had for the beginning.

THE DIRECTOR.
Yeah that's it
When you stand inside the brown hula hoop
And say
'I'm an arsehole'
That's brilliant
But I think at this point
We shouldn't let props do the work.

THE ACTOR.
Couldn't agree with you more.

THE DIRECTOR.
The beginning's going to be really brilliant
With the brown hula hoop.

She demonstrates.

THE ACTOR.
It was a terrific idea of yours.

THE DIRECTOR.
Uh-uh Dazza – your idea.

THE ACTOR.
Maybe in this bit we should have
Music in the background
Something very soft
Like in Death in Venice
Verdi I think it is.

THE DIRECTOR.
Yes the Adagietto from the Fifth Symphony

Actually it's Mahler
But I really don't think it's a good idea
I don't think you should try to reinforce
The mood of the text with music
Also if you play something by Mahler
And then say
I'm a piece of shit
People might think
We think the piece by Mahler
Is a piece of shit
That'd be stupid.

THE ACTOR.
But the line says that
I'm a piece of shit
People have got to understand
That means me and not the music.

THE DIRECTOR.
Yes.

THE ACTOR.
I think you're right that we ought to take
The audience seriously
And not think
They're stupider than they are.

THE DIRECTOR.
Ok I'm just going to go and have a look
In sound
I'm sure they'll have the Mahler.

THE DIRECTOR *exits.* THE ACTOR *is alone. He's not really sure what to do. First voice exercises. Peter Piper and so forth. Physical exercises. He fetches a brown hula hoop and swings it round his hips. Hums a note. Sings memememememe. Suddenly sings to an improvised tune: I'm a piece of shit. Runs to the door and shouts outside.*

THE ACTOR.
I know Claire
I've got it
I know
I'll sing it

To himself.

Then it'll be solved more through the form.

He cadges a cigarette from one of the audience, then a light and waits on stage, smoking. THE DIRECTOR *enters.*

THE DIRECTOR.
> They did have it
> In the sound department
> I'm just going to zip up to the box.

THE ACTOR.
> Hey I've got an idea
> I thought
> What about
> If I –
> Forget it.

THE DIRECTOR *takes the tape to the sound booth. Returns.*

THE DIRECTOR.
> Fergus was asleep
> Thought we'd finished.

THE ACTOR.
> Look I thought
> Instead of saying it
> I could sing it.

THE DIRECTOR.
> Right
> D'you think so
> It's just if we've got Mahler and you start singing
> Then it's quite clear
> It's the Mahler you mean
> Is a piece of shit.

THE ACTOR.
> I hadn't thought of that.
> You're right.

THE DIRECTOR.
> Let's give it a try
> With the Mahler
> I'm not certain

But we ought
To try it anyway

Loud.

So let's try this
With lights and sound
Darren's lying curled up on the table
– Darren lie down – and

Loud again.

The lights should take about thirty seconds to fade in
The sound needs to come in quite loud
Because the music is very quiet
Fergus can we hear a bar or two
Just to get a level.

The sound of Mahler's Fifth. Both listen. What a delightful picture of peace and harmony!

THE DIRECTOR.
It can come up a bit.

It is almost too loud. But what heavenly peace!

THE DIRECTOR.
That's nice
Let's just listen to it for a few more seconds
To get in the mood.

They listen for maybe thirty seconds.

THE DIRECTOR.
The lights should all be up by now
And then the text can come
Let's try it
It could be absolutely beautiful

Loud.

Ok that's enough
Lights out
Everyone ready
Lighting – sound – ok
Right I'll give you the cue

Softly.

Are you ready Darren.

THE ACTOR.
  Yes.

THE DIRECTOR.
  Good
  Now just concentrate
  For a couple of seconds.

  Pause.

THE DIRECTOR.
  And – cue.

  We hear 'Crucified' by Army of Lovers at full volume. THE DIRECTOR *shouts something in the dark. She leaps up, stumbles, falls. The stage is lit only very gradually.* THE ACTOR *is acting.*

THE DIRECTOR.
  Oi what the fuck's that supposed to be
  Ow
  That's wrong stop wrong
  Stop.

  THE ACTOR*'s lips are moving but we can't understand what he's saying. Neither can* THE DIRECTOR *who crawls, holding her knee, to the sound booth at the back of the stage. This takes a very long time. Now she's there. We can hear her arguing with someone.*

THE DIRECTOR.
  That's wrong – shit.

VOICE.
  What.

THE DIRECTOR.
  That's the wrong tape.

VOICE.
  What.

THE DIRECTOR.
  Turn it off.

VOICE.
  Why.

THE DIRECTOR.
Because it's the wrong tape.

VOICE.
What.

THE DIRECTOR.
It's the wrong one.

This small argument is repeated ad lib until THE DIRECTOR *manages to get inside the sound booth and the music is abruptly switched off.* THE ACTOR *is silent.* THE DIRECTOR *limps towards him.*

THE DIRECTOR.
I'm really sorry about that Darren.

THE ACTOR *stares.*

THE DIRECTOR.
What a mess
Darren
I'm really sorry for you
Darren
It must have been awful for you
I know.

THE ACTOR.
Let
Me
Try
It
Again
Please.

THE DIRECTOR.
Darren I don't understand
How that could have happened
I'll go back up there and show him
The tape again.

THE ACTOR *stares. He cries a little.* THE DIRECTOR *goes into the sound booth and comes back out again.*

THE DIRECTOR.
I think it would be really great
If you do it in the mood

You're in now
You don't need to do anything more
Just wait
Till the line comes out
I've told them
The lighting
Can take even longer
Forty seconds

Loud.

Lights out.

She is obeyed. Softly.

Are you ready Darren
Darren.

THE ACTOR.
Yes.

THE DIRECTOR.
Alright
Then lights and sound go.

We hear the Adagietto from Mahler's Fifth Symphony. The stage is lit very slowly. THE ACTOR *lies on stage very happy and relaxed. He smiles. Opens his mouth. Closes it again silently. Opens and closes it like a contented fish.*

THE DIRECTOR
(*very quietly and gently and of course very slowly*).
Now the line Darren
Now
You've got it now
Just say it.

THE ACTOR *smiles mute and content.*

THE DIRECTOR.
Say it Darren
I think it'll be really perfect
If you say it now.

THE ACTOR.
You know it was really great
When Malcolm told me

> I'd got the part
> The title role
> I didn't know
> What the play was called
> I think it's sweet
> That you're making such an effort
> But it's a bit silly
> Because on the first night I'm going to do
> What I want
> Me
> Whatever I want
> And I'm going to say
> Whatever I want
> I'll know
> What I am
> And I'm going to say so
> Me
> I'm.

THE DIRECTOR.
> Darren
> You are so on the right track there
> You're really responding
> To the text and the feelings
> That it's evoking inside you.

THE ACTOR.
> Anyway
> It's brilliant playing such a big part
> Where you can show so much of yourself
> Not just one colour
> An entire palette
> A big part helps you to forget things
> That life isn't
> The way you imagined it
> Disappointments
> I started off quite well
> I had promise
> Course I'm not good-looking enough
> For parts like Hamlet
> But lots of comedies

And now this here
It's a decent job
If people clap at the end
Simply because you learnt so many lines
Off by heart
That's right
It's depressing
But still you go back to the beginning and start again
Wanting to know
Wanting to forget past disappointments
Thinking that can't be it surely
On the first night
I'm going to do what I want
I'm going to say
I'm
And then
Whatever I think I
Am
And I'm definitely
Definitely not going to say
That I'm –

Lights up on the whole room.

THE DIRECTOR.
Darren
Let's leave it there for today shall we.

THE ACTOR *does not move.* THE DIRECTOR *sits in front of him, similarly still.*

The End.

JAMAICA

(*'Til Denver*)

a 'boulevard' comedy by
Oliver Bukowski

translated by David Spencer

'The worst direction that a story can take,
takes it into comedy'
(*F. Dürrenmatt*)

Oliver Bukowski was born in Cottbus in East Germany in 1961. His first play *Die Halbwertzeit der Kanarienvögel* had its first production in 1991 and played in various theatres throughout Germany. Other plays include: *London–LA–Lübbenau* (1992), *Intercity* (1993), *Bis Denver* (1995), *Goodbye Lucy Hello Lucy* (1996), *Nichts Schöneres* (1998) and *Gäste* (1999). His film *Bis Zum Horizont* was produced by Polyphon in 1998.

Translator's Notes

I've written the dialect speakers to the rhythm and slang of West Yorkshire. The notion of 'spell as it sounds' is faithful to the original. The dialect 'voice' of Ackers n'Pash is part of the undeclared socioeconomic debate of the drama, thus dialect must remain.

I choose this 'accent' because it's one I know; with a little effort, it should be possible to crack the code and set the play in any region of Great Britain - especially by simply letting native speakers of a particular accent some free space. This is to be encouraged.

The play is most certainly an East West debate in German, but has great parallels with the North South divide in Britain, since these geographical paradigms overlap significantly with political and social circumstances and in a similar manner in both 'lands' 'languages,' I don't see an over-riding requirement to set the play 'in Germany.' However, the producers of this version felt it was correct to retain the tune – the West German National Anthem – which Ackers has to sing on the bottle bank. If this tune feels awkward or forced – embedded as it is in dialect – use 'Land of Hope and Glory'.

Though I'm not in any way expert in English as it's spoken in other 'English' speaking countries, I suspect that in these lands too, there is a difference between the language of the proletariat, sub-proletariat, and the ruling class, which make this aspect of the play relevant.

'Bis Denver,' the play's original title, bases itself around a sound pun that one can do in German; 'Bis denn wa?' Which is sort of 'see you later eh?' In saying it as 'Bis Denver' it becomes 'until Denver' or 'at Denver.' In English we can say 'A'll be seeing yer' which moves to, 'A'l be sin yer' finally to 'Abyssinia.' I found that unsatisfactory, hence Jamaica, as in 'Did you make her' that moves to 'Ja make 'er?' Okay, a cringer of a joke, but 'true to the original!' Maybe other dialects present other solutions?

An Incomplete Glossary

A is I and sounded, 'ah'. Where I appears the 'I' is stressed.
Becuz, cuz, are because.
Cunt (apart from where it isn't) is could not.
Chuffed, pleased - particularly sexual.
Dunt is usually did not.
Meself is myself.
Nowt is nothing.
Owt is anything and sounded, 'out.'
Old Bill, the cops.
Summat is something and sounded, 'sum'at.'
Scoffing is eating.
Shagging is sexual intercourse.
X'zactly is exactly.

Mor' Chuffin' Noats

The use of ' is to encourage the compression of words, or to encourage the dropping of letter, say 'h's and 'g's as in 'He is sodding here!' ''E's soddin'ere!'

There are various systematic grammatical conventions, use of past tense where one might expect present, the reverse also.

The use of plurals where singulars might be expected, particularly on 'is' relate verbs, as in I were, meaning I was.

Don't slave to this; especially if it gets in the way of the conventions of another dialect.

And remember, a dialect is only a language without an army!

ANYWAY: There's lots more but the main points are these,

1) If you really like the play then why not cast people who can do the accent? 'Specially now a've gone tert trouble a writin' it all down.

2) Dialect is the colour of the play. Any dialect will bring its own colour; but without the dialect on the page then I wouldn't have translated Oliver's play, I would have merely presented a black and white sketch of a fabulously colourful romp!

Jamaica ('Til Denver) was first performed in English as a rehearsed reading in the *New German Voices* season in the Theatre Upstairs on 4 December 1997 with the following cast:

TERRE	Bruce Alexander
INA TERRE	Susan Brown
PASCHKE	David Ross
ACKERMANN	Barry Stanton

Director Roxana Silbert
Translator David Spencer

Characters

HORST PASCHKE, *known also as 'Pasch'*
LOTHAR ACKERMANN, *known also as 'Ackers'*
TERRE
INA TERRE
THOMAS TERRE

The latter of these, for the duration, is a corpse; but also a centre, an axis, a kind of black hole between the social world of the Terre's and Ackers n'Pash, thus the main part (!) – that means: NO DOLL!

Paschke speaks 'originally' Niederlausitz, a dialect from a mainly rural area of the former German Democratic Republic (GDR. DDR.)

Ackermann speaks Berlinerish.

Notes to the Text

/ is a pause, change in tack, the space to think, to react, to solicit non verbal response. An actor's reading should take it as a sort of 'Ah ha!?'

CAPITALS don't always mean shout, but they do always suggest intensity or emphasis.

Scene One

ACKERMANN *and* PASCHKE *at a lacklustre shooting-gallery.* PASCHKE *necks ale from a can; he's full steaming pissed and strung up from head to toe with pig-shit-stupid-snick-snack prizes.* ACKERMANN *shoots and smokes; at points of maximum concentration he clamps his glowing fag behind his ear.*

PASCHKE (*opens his gob, belches endlessly*). . . . . intellect! / As a were saying . . . Becuz . . . The most desolate of deserts. The abs'ha'lute steppe. Is when intellect duz like it can organize owt. / Listen. Ackers. In the Age of Enlightenment the Protistan . . . Proto'stan . . . Protestant Church needed wot they call Revivalists . . . they'd bloody great poles. And they'd pitchfork their way through the congregation. Stopping 'em from sleeping. Listen! REVIVALISTS! / That Ackers. Is how it is. / In general philosophy is bullshit. And specifically. Philosophy's there so as we've got summat t'do between scoffing and shagging. Y'get me? Cuz us humans. Cuz we can't be shagging and scoffing all the time. So we do a bit of philosophy. / Nay Ackers! We're nowt better. Nowt higher. Just cuz we think we can think we're thinking. And on top of that. Who sez . . . who sez Vivi'aldi. Or fer that matter Einstein. Or yer shite Joyce. Who sez that they did summat higher than say . . . say . . for example . . . (PASCHKE *spies his beer can.*) The inventer of the beer tin! Eh? Who sez that then!?

ACKERMANN (*without turning*). You got anymore quid coins?

PASCHKE (*he carries out an elaborate search*). Nay Ackers. Nay. Let me tell you summat. All that Ulysses research. All that Quantum Theory. All that Ulysses stuff and fifty. Never mind fifty. Say a'undred-and-fifty bloody Quantum

Theories. It don't change yer dead normal. Call it what y'like. Private Ackers'-Actuality. It don't change it anything like say three simple six-packs. / Or a straight-forward spot on yer thigh. / How it is Ackers? How? / We can't be Creation's ultimate! Humanity. No way. Us. We are a pile of shite some pisshead blew life into! Look at yerself. Right at yerself. Starkers in the mirror. Do you really think y'the perfect model? You? With yer rubber-ring'o gut-blubber. Yer warts and yer pathetic bit a dick dangling. Nay. Yer average dromedary looks smarter than you or me. A lot smarter! / Dromedary? / How did a get on to one humped camels? (*Drinks.*) Bollocks.

ACKERMANN. A pair a pink ash-trays or five Kennedy salt-pots?

PASCHKE. Kennedy?

ACKERMANN. Salt pours out a'the bullet-hole. So sez baldyman (*The shooting gallery owner.*) over there.

PASCHKE. Wat would we do with five salt-pots?

ACKERMANN (*into the gallery*). The ashtrays!

ACKERMANN *gives the ashtrays to* PASCHKE.

PASCHKE. Anyway. / Sirius. D'yer get me? / Say you're intelligent life Ackers. Just for the sake of example. You're intelligent life on Sirius. Y'get me? Let me tell you what y'do! As an inti . . . an intelly . . . an in-tell-lectual. Do y'know what?

ACKERMANN (*into the gallery*). That target's hit baldyman! Don't try and take the piss out of me! Hit's hit!.

PASCHKE. What y'do is a spek . . . a spick . . . a spectral analysis. From our lovley mum. The Milky-way! Yer instructaments. They're state a the art lad. The slightest difference in temperature is converted to one of million colours. You can miss nowt. / But you. Yer sat there in front a yer instructaments. Fucked off. Bugger all t'do. Get me? Bored! So bored y'poke one of yer fifteen arseholes. Could be? Do you know how many aresholes they've got on Sirius. Do yer? So yer poking. Listen Ackers. And then it happens. Us. All of this and us here. Our Earth. Somehow we crash into summat. WHAM! THE END. / NOWT N'MORE! / And you? What do you do? With yer fifteen pairs a goggle-eyes. I mean. Who knows what they look like on Sirius. It could be Ackers. That yer dick's an electra-magnetic-force-field. And yer eyeballs aren't in yer face but in yer liver! Could be. Eh? With a bit of imagination. / So there you are Ackers. Yer fifteen livers gawping at all of creation. And wàt y'see? After The Big Blue Marble's gone for good from under us bum!? All of us gone for good? What d'yer see Ackers? NOWT! Y'see Sweet Fanny Adams! Y'turn off yer instructaments. An' bugger off 'ome t'stick yer 'lectra-magnetic-force-field into the ear of 'yer Sirius Wife. / A mean. It could be the birds on Sirius shag with their ears. Imagine it! Eh? / No? So anyway. Despite all yer state of the art ins . . . instructa . . . instruments. Y'see nowt! / A read it. 'Even in the case of total destruction of planet Earth. Seen spick-tra-lee-anaa-lyt-ic-lee. There would be no noticeable change in the colour spectrum of the Milky-way.' Listen! Galactically. We're no more than pickled micro'scop'ic onions. S'much so . . . (*An expansive gesture that's intended to take in all creation.*) . . . that this lot. THE WHOLE LOT! Could blow up. And that slag of a Milky-way. She wunt even blush up a bit red. As this . . . (*Repeats his expansive gesture.*) . . . as this whole lot gets flushed down the interstellar bog. (*Laughs and drinks.*)

ACKERMANN (*into the gallery*). 'Oh! Oh!' Have a got me nose in me arse or what? Let a toothless Pope suck me bollocks dry. (*Continues shooting; amused, to himself.*) 'Oh oh oh.' Man! What an arse'ole!

PASCHKE (*ponders*). And' X'ZACTLY. X'ZACTLY THAT. Is what you have t'do. T'view all of this as though yer seeing from Sirius. ALL OF IT ACKERS! That's the solution. THAT is the solution!

If possible, ACKERMANN *gives an enormous stuffed animal to* PASCHKE, *so enormous that no shooting gallery could ever house it. The giving and the receiving are part of a complex ritual. Neither business or speech are affected. It's the pisshead's routine acquaintance with the abnormal.*

PASCHKE. Viewed from Sirius. All of it down here is baked-beans. Up there. It makes no difference if you have t'stand on a bin and sing 'For Us German Fatherland.'

ACKERMANN. Wat fer'a bin?

PASCHKE. It makes no difference! / Want more quid coins? (*Digs in his pockets.*) Am out of 'em.

ACKERMANN. Am asking yer. What bin? And what. F'fucksake. For a song!?

PASCHKE. A. A bottle bank.

ACKERMANN. Bottle bank?

PASCHKE. A think and a . . . (*To the tune of the German National Anthem.*) La La La La La . . .

ACKERMANN. For us German fatherland? (PASCHKE *nods gravely.*)

PASCHKE. Viewed from Sirius . . .

ACKERMANN. And what kind'a pig thick sod. Stands on a bin. T'sing such shite. / Yer babblin! Yer boozin! Babblin' n'boozin'. Very out of the usual for *you*. 'Bin!'

PASCHKE *silent.* ACKERMANN *shoots.*

PASCHKE. Aye well!? . . . If I'd a got me way . . .

ACKERMANN. You? You made someone stand on a bin . . . / Or were it you? Pissed? God knows what it's good for. But I can believe it! You. Standing on a bin bawling out yer lungs. Must have been a hell of a party. (*Fakes envy.*) I should have been invited!

PASCHKE. It would'a been easier if I'd had a skinful.

ACKERMANN. Y'weren't pissed? / Totally sober. You mount a bottle-bank. And have a singsong?

PASCHKE. A were grabbed! They shoved me up on it. At first a were t'sing whilst a'were wanking. But it sickened them. Me not being the youngest no more . . . It weren't so bad *anyway.* Nowt else happened. A mean. They could have done a lot of other stuff. Weird stuff. / There's a lot of about it these days. Eh? . . . Me Ackers. Me. A dunt give a toss . . . WHO ARE WE THEN. Eh? / We dunt let it . . .

ACKERMANN. WHO!? WHO WAS IT!?

PASCHKE (*after a pause*). Four of 'em.

ACKERMANN. Four? / Would y'know 'em?

PASCHKE. Never forget 'em! Drag me out a me sleep. In the middle of the night. I'd know 'em. / One of 'em. He had sortov blond hair. Holger they called him . . . Holger or Olaf or . . . / Anyroad. Four of 'em. One looked like young Terre. Y'know? Very smart clothes. Dead clean like. *Normal.*

ACKERMANN (*kicks against the gallery*). The . . . bloody swines!

PASCHKE (*trying to calm his panic*). Akers . . . have they now? In the end like . . . A mean. Have I now been . . . were I . . . am I raped? Eh? Y'can't say. A don't think. A mean. An Anthem's just an Anthem. So why shouldn't yer sing it from the top of a bottle-bank? / And anyway. On top a that. They were only youths. Young lads are young lads. Eh? They have their fun fer christsakes. And did they laugh? / A mean. You ever heard a that. Someone doing a rape. And laughing? / Nay. It dunt fit at all. It dunt fit at all. Eh?

ACKERMANN *takes hold of* PASCHKE's *arm.*

ACKERMANN. Yer alright Pash. It's alright. It were only a bit o'fun. A joke. 'Viewed' from Syphilis.

PASCHKE. Sirius.

ACKERMANN. What a sed.

Scene Two

PASCHKE *smokes and drinks as he works with scissors and glue on the first blackmail letter of his life.*

PASCHKE (*nags the corpse*) . . . not *my* . . . I couldn't help it. If you. With yer slag. Y'hear me? / Never mind that! It's a children's pond. A bloody half-way natural pond fer kiddies. For the last bloody time! It's there fer bloody brats. A night too me'lad. Fer kiddies. And not f'you and yer stupid

junk! / Every bloody morning me. I'd yer shite Johnnies
t'gather up. Spunked in. Filth . . . / Hunderd thousand. Do
yer reckon yer Paps is worth s'much? What's a Professor
make? Loads a money. Safe bet we him writing stuff f'them
Sundey Supplements. 'An word with the Professor.' Ethics?
/ Aye well. Wat dew I know? What Ethics brings in? He pay
up. Old Man Terre. Fer his fancy Master Terre . . . Christsakes. A need a zero. / (*Rummages through the magazines.*)
Must be a'nuther zero somewhere. / Aye. And yer bloody
syringes. Yer leave them lying about and all. IN MY POOL!
The gammy things. And were I t'miss one. Then some kiddy.
IN MY POOL. Gets a full dose of yer AIDs. Yer Cholera.
Yer Bullimia. Yer five a'clock shadow. And whatever other
plagues-a-lurgie lurk in yer blood. And it's me. Mr Horst
Paschke. Gets a buggering at her Majesty's pleasure. And
all of that. Cuz you have t'have yer shite-night-parties in my
pool. / (*Reads his note.*) ' . . . wait for yer at 13.15 by the
telephone box on the corner of Cho'pin and Moat'hart street.'
Moats'hart. Now d'yer spell that (O.T.E.) Oh tea E. Or
(O.A.T.) oh ay tea. Moats'hart? Moats'hart. (*Drinks.*) And
(H.A.R.) wi' need f'sure. Haytch ay aar. 'aytch hay aar.
'aytch hay aar. 'aytch hay aar. (*Reads a caption.*) 'Hardcore
in the classroom. School-girl seduction. Hot and tab'bew'less.'
/ Wat mut Ackers collects. Well anyroads. Haytch hay aar
owttert hardcore will dew me. 'Moats'hart.' / And top of it
all. Yer must of seen't sign. 'Danger! No bathing beyond the
Safety Line!' It's written big n'clear. / But that's how your
lot is. In't it? Nowts sacred. All yer good for is scoffing.
Supping. N'shaggin'. . . Joyriding with yer Old Man's
Ethic-Porsche. And scoffing. Supping. N'shagging. Let me
tell yew something. Even if you've loads a back handed
cash from yer fancy family. / Yer still the shitest of shites.
Every Binman. Every street-sweeper. Aye. Even little Life-
Guards of little puddles fer little kiddies. Listen. Every little
life-guard is a thousand . . . a hundred-thousand times more
werth than you. So you've no need t'goggle so arrogant.
(*Comes to his senses.*) Aye well. A can at least close yer
eye-balls. That's what y'do in't it. Eh?

ACKERMANN *makes a noise, trying to open the door from outside.*

JAMAICA 111

ACKERMANN. Paschke! Damm n'buggering blast it! Why've yer locked-up. Are y'giving Mona one or what?

PASCHKE (*a mad panic of tidying*). Shite! Shite! Shite! / Ackers . . . am cummin like. Just-a-second. Second.

ACKERMANN. Knew it. You've blew up Mona and made night of it! But yer in for aggro now pal! (*Bashes the door.*) Big time!

PASCHKE. Man! (*Drags away the body, quietly.*) Do you have t'be so heavy. / Ackers? A weren't doing Mona. A were sleeping.

ACKERMANN. Y'don't believe that yerself.

PASCHKE *opens up.*

PASCHKE. Are y'right Ackers?

ACKERMANN. State of here! Where is she? Am telling yer. You'll scrub her snow-white. If you've shot yer load in . . .

PASCHKE. Ackers. If you want?

ACKERMANN. Pash!? / They're wet and . . .

PASCHKE. I'll get yer new ones.

ACKERMANN. Pash! THESE ARE MY MAGS!

PASCHKE. A sodding sex-shop full.

ACKERMANN. All of 'em! All of 'em! Cut t'bits!? Y'daft get! Any idea what these things cost? This! Ten ninety nine! Here. Twelve ninety ninety. 'Playmates In Paradise.' / Yew've mutilated half a'Blondie's arse! / Horst! Out of order! Good! We can share us mincemeat. But y'keep yer paws off my literature. Everyone has a right to a bit a night life. Literally.

PASCHKE. You'll get brand new literature. And on top a that. A'll treat yer. Twice?

ACKERMANN. We're talking the full Thai Massage here? / Four.

PASCHKE. Three.

ACKERMANN. Done! / But Pash! It's the full works. The full bloody programme!

PASCHKE. It's booked!

ACKERMANN. And where the hell will you get the money for it. Eh?

PASCHKE. My business.

ACKERMANN. And when?

PASCHKE. Soon. Very soon. Before you know it they'll be trampling on yer balls.

ACKERMANN. If this is just flannel . . .

PASCHKE. Flannel? Listen. A dozen tins a Red Stripe sez I mean it! And you get mincemeat 'til yer rip yer kecks!

ACKERMANN. Oh aye?

PASCHKE. And fer two whole weeks. I was these yellow stained things.

ACKERMANN. My undies? Fuckssake Pash. That's nowt t'joke about!

PASCHKE. What y'gotta do y'gotta do!

PASCHKE gives ACKERMANN his hand, seals the deal.

Scene Three

Slightly later, ACKERMANN *and* PASCHKE *in their 'pyjamas.'*

ACKERMANN. Oh no! Oh no! / Pour us another!!! Nay. / Oh man.

PASCHKE. What were y'doing rooting under't bed anyway?

ACKERMANN. Pasch. That's it. It. A tell yer. Mad? You've gone ballistic.

PASCHKE. A'd a kept you out of it.!

ACKERMANN. Oh no! No way. Nay! / Yer an arsehole Pasch. Headcase. Y'know at first I thought it were a new Mona. A were only searching for me slippers! And BANG! A did. A thought it were a new Mona. A were just thinking. 'Ackers lad y'should give it one!' Just got me down! And! It's a corpse. Deader then dead! / You know you nearly made a necro'fileo'faxer outta me. / No way. / Pour us another. / Right? Carry on.

PASCHKE. Aye well as all'ways. As y'know.

ACKERMANN. Young Terre's driven up with his Porsche? Then what?

PASCHKE. Him and his slag get owt. She's driving a similar wagon. And then. / Well. As y'know. They get to it. And after a while. Bang in't middle. They stop rutting. And the slag puts her 'what do you think I am' look on. And gets in her car.

ACKERMANN. Likes t'shit-stab does young Terre.

PASCHKE. Aye. He even looks full bloody anal. / Anyhow. Soon as the slags gone. Young Terre flings himself inter't pond.

ACKERMANN. Suicide?

PASCHKE. Australian crawl.

ACKERMANN. Australian who? A thought he drown?

PASCHKE. Well er . . .

ACKERMANN. Well what?

PASCHKE. Then it happened.

ACKERMANN. Godssake Pasch! WHAT HAPPENED! And don't tell me a bloody shark. Or that the Australian crawled into a buoy!?

PASCHKE. Just like that. (*Makes a slurping sound.*) He were gone.

ACKERMANN. Just like that?

PASCHKE. Just like that!

ACKERMANN. A. (*Mimics the slurping sound.*) And he were gone.

PASCHKE. Yep.

ACKERMANN. / Pasch? I've an idea. A. (*Again the slurping sound.*) And he were drown?

PASCHKE. Yep.

ACKERMANN. You wunt mind telling me WHERE that 'appened? It couldn't well. Co-incidentally. It couldn't be beyond the safety line?

PASCHKE. The red n'white wun.

ACKERMANN. To-tal-ley co-in-cidentally? Right next to the the fresh-water pump and drain?

PASCHKE. / Well as you said Ackers. The likes and sort of young Terre. They're complete shite. The likes of Terre. So you said. His like puts our like. Up on the bottle-bank.

ACKERMANN. Right! I get yer! / And you. You sortov scooped the complete shite. As if he were some floating dog turd. From the surface. And so to speak. Flushed it down the bog.

PASCHKE. Not quite. / A just didn't turn off the drainage-pump. / Not straight off. A just wanted to give him a bit of a fright! That nice little lad. My god! / You know I can't get (*To the tune.*) 'Freedom, Law and Unity' out of me head?

ACKERMANN. Frighten him? Boo boo like? / PASH YOU BLOODY IDIOT! You're a full bloody murderer.

PASCHKE. Well a . . .

ACKERMANN. Well a!? / Well a!!! / Right! Alright. Now then. You tell me. What else are you? I mean if yer not a mean dog murdering swine! Disguised as a lifeguard.

PASCHKE (*tuts*). . . . It could be fate what did it? Could be. Fate and God. In the end who knows?

ACKERMANN. You're not telling me it were God's will?

PASCHKE. Well. Could be. X'zactly. The will of the Lord. / But . . .

ACKERMANN. But?

PASCHKE. Then again it could have been the drainage pump.

ACKERMANN. Yep. / The . . . / A can't fathom it! Are you saying we've t'take us hat off. And pray to the drainage pump. HORST PASCHKE'S LORD GOD ALMIGHTY! / It dunt sound so bad!? / Have y'packed yer toothbrush?

PASCHKE. Hey! That there Terre's only shaped from the same shite as his Old Man. That! Y'can take as booked. That's the manners you get from money! So you said. 'The whole family is of totally mouldy character!'

ACKERMANN. Yes. As far as am concerned. But? What's gonna happen next? A mean. Have yer phoned up?

PASCHKE. Well a was thinking of writing a note.

ACKERMANN. Ohw nice one! A little postcard. 'Dear Cops. I've just drown someone. The foods shite but me and Ronnie Biggs are best of mates. The weather's good. Your sincerely Horttie Paschke.' / Man! Listen! They put a reward out for yer! They'll do one a them artists impri'sessions. It'll go all over't world! They'll have bounty hunters on yer back! Especially since young Terre were such a famous twat. / Have yer teld the cops or what?

PASCHKE. Why tell the cops? That can't help young Terre now. No. It were his Old Man a were thinking of writing to.

ACKERMANN. His Old Man? / Oh. You think I'm stupid don't yer! / You were gonna fake loony like. Get 'diminished responsibility?' Very clever! / If you want my help. I'll tell 'em. Pash? He's nowt upstairs. A complete bungalow. I'll tell 'em you shampooed with toilet cleaner. Or that you wanked off with pictures of a Polar Bear. The one off the *Fox's Glacier Mints*. Or a . . . / A'll say yer what you liked t'do most were to be up on a bottle bin. Bawling out 'For Us German Fatherland!' You've enough witnesses for that! Seeing as you love to do it most in the middle of rush hour.

PASCHKE. Ackers!? Ackers. A know y'wannabe a nice bloke. You'll never make it. And do you know why? Cuz yer not colouring with a full set crayons. Strain yerself. Think! See the total spectrum. A mean he's dead now anyway . . . get me? Dead and rich as hell . . . And us Ackers. What are we?

ACKERMANN. Aliver for one thing!

PASCHKE. Yeah. And? AND? Can you shop with that? / In this case. Let me tell you. Mr Horst Paschke is. For the last time Mr Horst Paschke the object of pisstakers! NO MORE MISTER NICE GUY! Horst Paschke is now doing himself a slice the pie. And finished.

ACKERMANN. You what! Pasch! Brother. About face! It's not for the likes us. No way! / Okay. Nicking the odd six-pack. Screwing the odd Automat! In order. But that Pasch! Listen! That sets off all the bloody sirens! One for the headlines. I can see it. 'Horst the Flusher!' 'The Monster from Kiddypool Lagoon!' 'Paschke. As gruesome as his name!' / Gimmie a break!

PASCHKE. And for what? WHAT FOR? For what were we made Ackers? In another fifteen. At most twenty years. We'll both be just a sack full of maggots. / We're getting older! Just the other day. They got up on't bus. T'give us a seat! / Ackers. Boozers like us. Those who think and do like we think and do. They can only go by the name of Lothar Ackermann n'Horst Paschke. We are grey from the dole. Yellow with seriosis of the liver. And obese from fish-cakes and mincemeat. / We've nowt t'lose?

ACKERMANN. INHUMAN! SICK! PEVERSE! And . . . Although . . . A mean. In the end. It was *only an accident*.

PASCHKE. X'zactly. We do little Tezza for all he's worth. 'Til stones bleed. We get us-selves a little stash. Then we're off. (*Fills the glasses.*) Now. Me plan's this. First-off. We need a new freezer. Second . . .

ACKERMANN. A new freezer? That'll cost us at least half-a-grand.

PASCHKE. Little Terre dunt fit in us old one. I've tried squashing him in. But there was always some bit what stuck out.

ACKERMANN. Could be but. A new freezer? Straight away? A mean. What if we ask Big Dieter. He's bound to have a chain-saw. (*Does a chain-saw.*) Rummm two three four. And young Terre's goulash.

PASCHKE. Standards Lothar. Wer not that sort.

ACKERMANN. But straight away a new deep-freeze . . .

PASCHKE. Investment. Start capital! You don't get out fer nowt.

They toast.

Scene Four

TERRE *senior and his wife sit opposite each other in silence; they're taking their evening meal, of laughably small servings. After a while.*

TERRE. Did I . . . (*Together.*)

INA TERRE. When you . . .

TERRE (*laughs*). You first.

INA TERRE. Not so important. You first.

TERRE. It's important to me. Everything you say. Every word. I'm listening.

INA TERRE. Sweet of you but. It really wasn't anything special.

TERRE. Don't have me drag it out of you.

INA TERRE. Well . . . I . . . / Whoops. *Forgotten.* (*Laughs.*) You see. It can't have been anything especially pertinent.

TERRE. And? Is it to your taste?

INA TERRE. Totally delicious. Totally delicious. You cook like a God.

TERRE. Such a compliment. In its absence. Would certainly have been impertinent. After all, I was a full two hours in the kitchen.

INA TERRE. But perhaps? It wasn't at all my intention. To praise you. Perhaps . . .

TERRE. Ah? So? Not to your liking. You almost certainly find it insipid.

INA TERRE. Certainly not. Not at all.

TERRE. Then I don't understand. Why for you. A few plain words of recognition are too much.

INA TERRE. But I already praised the soup starter . . .

TERRE. Yes. 'It smells fantastic.' Nothing more. / Darling. Should it have passed you by. We're already on our second main course.

INA TERRE. I . . . I am sorry . . .

TERRE. No bother.

INA TERRE. No. You're totally right. I was so enjoying it that there was nothing more to . . .

TERRE. A nuance too . . . too demagogic don't you think?

INA TERRE. I was just about to . . . just about . . . to say . . .

TERRE. Yes?

INA TERRE (*feverishly reconsiders, then relieved*). The salt. I merely wanted to ask. If there's salt.

TERRE (*holding back*). Salt?

INA TERRE (*realizes the mistake*). What? . . . Oh what an idiot I am. The wine. I meant. I wanted another sip from that wonderful . . .

TERRE. But your glass is full to the brim.

INA TERRE. But I eventually. I would have surely soon . . .

TERRE (*to himself*). The salt. Then it was. Insipid. No matter what I do my darling will always find some fault. Not easy. Really not easy.

INA TERRE. Anyhow. The fish was fantastic.

TERRE. And the game!? Insipid.

INA TERRE. I didn't . . . ehm . . . I. I could eat a whole bowlfull of your venison.

TERRE. The thought alone I find disgusting but. Please. If it's your wish. Here. Have my portion. (*Unloads the meat from his plate onto hers.*) I've certainly. I think. Taken too much.

INA TERRE. If I wasn't already so full. I mean. I could explode. I'm so full.

TERRE (*repulsed*). 'Explode?'

INA TERRE (*laughs, then submissively*). Again? Another not such a well chosen metaphor. True?

TERRE. My darling. You now have the chance to demonstrate. That your anthem to the *sauté* is an elevation beyond the rhetorical. *Bon appetit.*

She takes the plate and bravely starts to eat. He watches her, nervously.

TERRE. What . . . is smacking?

INA TERRE (*mouth full*). Pardon? (*Swallows swiftly.*) Pardon?

TERRE. When you chew. You smack. Such a slight sound. Lingering in the background. One could go mad. Don't you hear it too?

INA TERRE. I'm . . . Excuse me. I . . .

TERRE. No. No. It's not your fault. Who knows? (*Laughs.*) Who knows what sounds I MYSELF secrete. Just simply do as if said nothing. Please. (*Bids her to continue.*) I like to watch you.

INA TERRE *puts a morsel in her mouth; her attempts to eat, silently, develop into a slap-stick number. Eventually she coughs, chokes, and coughs. She puts a napkin in front of her mouth, but not quickly enough.* TERRE, '*concerned*', *goes to her and pats her back, carefully.*

TERRE. Dear dear. *Un petit malheur?* / We'll soon clear that up. (*Picks up some of what she has spat out; she stiffens.*) What do we have here? A mite of meat. Woof. Gone. And here. What can that have been? Vegetable? Artichoke perhaps? Hum. Looks more like an asparagus head. What do you think? / Somehow it always makes me consider. I mean. When one observes the results of a carefully prepared meal. As soon as it's had contact with the apparatus of food consumption. The tongue. The amalyse of our saliva. The aesthetics of destruction. Have I missed some small sweet scrap?

INA TERRE (*quiet*). On the vase.

TERRE. Pardon?

INA TERRE. VASE! (*Cynically.*) Stuck on the vase. There's a small shred of meat. With a sweet trace of gum-blood. Your favourite of favourites.

TERRE. Oh? I haven't in some manner aroused my little woman's indignation? It seems I just can't help it.

INA TERRE (*silent a moment, controlled*). Yes. He is. MY SON. And yes he has a few of your credit cards . . .

TERRE. Nine darling nine!

INA TERRE. Nine of 'your' cards? Nine if you so wish.

TERRE. 'If you so wish.' (*Short sniff.*) Inga-Lore!

INA TERRE. Don't call me Inga-Lore!

TERRE. 'If you so wish?' Ina. 'If you so wish?' / But even with my best of wishes. He remains the prime suspect. And he is I am afraid. . . .

TERRE *and* INA TERRE. Not the material excellence of MY inheritance.

INA TERRE. / I know. I know. But he is still . . .

TERRE *and* INA TERRE. Only half a child.

TERRE. / He's twenty seven. And uses the expertise obtained in his legal training. Training financed by MYSELF. Uses said expertise to send his own father temporary orders of injunction! Whilst simultaneously keeping himself occupied by driving my Porsche and filling up brand name condoms in teenagers. 'Only half a child.'

INA TERRE. You're a monster!

TERRE. Wasn't it only the other day he grabbed your bum in the bath!

INA TERRE (*crying*). No. He just wanted to . . . stroke. Stroke his mother. Stroke her.

TERRE. Then it's not so easy to understand. Why you. Socked his ear-hole for it.

INA TERRE. I . . . I a . . . misunderstood him. Anyway . . . anyway. It was my back. More my back he wanted to . . .

TERRE (*poisonous laugh*). Yes. Your back. MORE YOUR BACK! / Do you know what he does? Do you!? / Our little lover-of-mother's-back-sonny-boy. Blasts down to the baby-market. And I don't mean the toy shop! He loads up the car with pre-pubescents. / Are you sitting comfortably? Then he drives them to some children's swimming pool. He spends his days at the children's pool. Do you hear me? A CHILDREN's pool and . . .

INA TERRE. Stop it!!! Stop it!!!

TERRE. I've had him watched.

INA TERRE (*hate-filled*). Exactly!!! Exactly! That's you. Had him watched. Had. Had. Had . . . Do you know what you are? An ugly fat old pig. You . . . You . . . You ACADEMIC you!

INA TERRE *breaks into tears.* TERRE *goes to her and strokes her head. With his other hand he opens his flies. He, eventually, ejaculates into her mouth, and turns away from her.*

TERRE. We do love each other. Truly we do!?

She nods. She sits there. Her mouth full. Nearly crazy with disgust.

Why don't you swallow it down then? You always swallow it down. Like walnuts you say. Like walnuts. The taste of my sperm. Usually. You've always enjoyed the taste.

She swallows it.

Scene Five

Sinking the Porsche in the lake-side pool.

ACKERMANN. . . . I took right good care of me scooter. It were the high point of me life. A tinkered her everyday. Screwin'. Doing what had t'be done. A chromed up the mud-guards. Sprayed the Canadian flag on her body-werk. It looked ace!

PASCHKE. Canada? What have you got t'do wi'Canada?

ACKERMANN. A'd only a maple-leaf template.

PASCHKE. Anyway. That Porsche's gotta go beyond the line! And then if we keep the pump on all day. Nobody'll go near it.

ACKERMANN. What, you'll keep the pump on all day? Pasch! We'll have another corpse by dinner. Have y'gone blood-lust or what?

PASCHKE. It's gotta go.

ACKERMANN. It were me scooter's fault. For me first time inside.

PASCHKE. Riding it pissed?

ACKERMANN. Nooh! Bloody cyclist! Ran smack into me. Put a dent straight through Canada! A leapt off. And kicked in what were left of his head. (*Shows.*) A cracked his skull from there t'there. / Did a year and two months we good behaviour. When a got out Yennifa had seld it. T'buy a push-chair. Bloody cow. / A do a year and two months. For a bloody push-chair!

PASCHKE. Hey? Let's get it done. It's nearly bloody dawn.

ACKERMANN. We could just take her for a little spin? Pasch? Just once. Once 'round pond. Just look at the body work! 'Lectric windows. Air bags. Turbo. Air-conditionin' . . .

PASCHKE. Nooh way. / Yer pissed! And drunk-driving can wreck lives. A mean. It wouldn't be right t'go over the top. Make a serial killer of yerself? Eh? / Am cold. We've been sat here all bloody night.

ACKERMANN. Fair enough. Not x'zactly a whale of a wake. Is it? Can't remember the last time a were so pissed off. / Just once 'round t' pond. Just once. So I know why I've lived? And it'll be revenge like. For me scooter!

PASCHKE. A do understand yer. As I were a lad. We'd foals. We trained 'em. Looked after 'em. Morning to night. A cunt leave 'em alone. / Then one dawn. They were gone. A dint even say good bye. Sold to some frog fer franks. That were me first brush we international capital! Horsemeat.

ACKERMANN. Let's just get it in the water. Eh? So if we never once rode in a Porsche. No big deal is it PASCH! EH?

PASCHKE. Don't be a bloody bungalow! That Porsche is not worth a bloody man's life. And life's what I could get if they find it.

ACKERMANN. My life's worth about as much as a second-hand bike. Or a clapped-out rust-box. Where you have t'put yer feet through't floor and peddle like Freddie Flintstone.

PASCHKE. You shunt run yerself down.

ACKERMANN. Y'mean put meself down! Put not run!

PASCHKE. Even if it's true y'shouldn't say it. / Let's face it. About the likes of that Porsche. A've me ideas too. 'Horst lad.' A thinks. 'What kind of crapped up water closet are yer?' / My day will come. It will definitely come! / It will!

ACKERMANN. Faith is a blessing! / Me. Me like. A say the same. There must be. At some point in life. An amnesty from life's Shite! / And then a see that bloody machine. That car there. And I say. MY DAY HAS COME! asch. Am begging. Once 'round the pond! Eh?

PASCHKE. Us tew. We dunt fit in the like a that. (*Gets up.*) Cum on.

ACKERMANN. Objection PASH!

PASCHKE *gives him a hard stare.*

ACKERMANN. Alright. Am yer partner. A'll do me part. / (*Mumbles.*) But nub'dey better tell me there's any pity left in't world!

Scene Six

ACKERMANN *and* PASCHKE, *in disguise, near the appointed telephone booth.* PASCHKE *tries to hold back his giggles.*

ACKERMANN. What you gawping at? Y'daft twat! Whatever my Yenny were. She always said my head were made fer hats! Like that fella outta 'Casablanca'. So she sed. Anyroad y'can't tell me your mush looks 'ny better? A bloody egg wi' pubic hair!

PASCHKE. A dint wanna insult yer.

ACKERMANN. You've no bloody idea. Him outta 'Casablanca'. That's me! / They're half an hour late.

PASCHKE. / They'll come. They'll come. And without the cops! They'll have to. They're nowt but a bunch of bandits themselves. They want no bother with the Bobbies. / They'll cough up. / Can yer take me paper.

ACKERMANN. Pasch!? First y'bought a magazine. Not a paper. Second. We've already swopped us readables three times. And third. God knows what drove yer t'buy it. The bloody 'Rubber & Laytex Directory'.

PASCHKE. SUSH!

ACKERMANN. / Oh. The Grannie there.

PASCHKE. Could be a disguise.

ACKERMANN. A Grannie? That int a disguise. 'Specially not wi' such a caved-in-gob-of-a-dog. (*Checks her out.*) God!? It looks like it's been in a crash-test.

PASCHKE. Peek'a'knees. / And the handbag? She wunt leave a bloody great handbag just standing there. No real Grannie would do a thing like that!

ACKERMANN. / Could it be she's Al'zheimer?

PASCHKE. A don't give a shit about what she's called. It's the bag what matters . . . Look! She just lets it stand there. Am telling yer. That whole bloody Grannie act's nowt but a cover.

ACKERMANN. Y'reckon?

PASCHKE. Right! We slide over there. Have a little chat. Dead normal. Like nowt's on. Then we come back here. And then we do it all again. The whole thing. Three times. Then WHAM! Grab the bag and off! Ditch us masks under't bridge. Pack out the cash.

PASCHKE. And. (*Whistles 'casual'.*) Away we go. Dead normal. Wi'the train! Like pigs in shite!

ACKERMANN. A dunno. / A can't just think of ought. Not just like that. A mean. What's dead normal? What am a gunna say?

PASCHKE. Don't start! Just say whatever . . . Whatever comes into head. There must be summat y'know summat about?

ACKERMANN (*moronic laugh*). Oh aye.

PASCHKE. What's chuffed yew? Found a shiny button or what?

ACKERMANN. A reckon that Grannie's gonna light up when she hears me going on about shagging!

PASCHKE. LISTEN! / Not a word about shagging! Summat normal's what a said.

ACKERMANN. Shagging's normal.

PASCHKE. No it int.

ACKERMANN. That you'd go Catholic with old age . . .

PASCHKE. . . . God! There's such a thing as a situation.

ACKERMANN. Not for me! A could always manage an hard on.

PASCHKE. . . .?

ACKERMANN. All am sayin is. / There ain't a single film. Wer sum stupid get does a deal wi'some Grannie. Not wun!

PASCHKE (*stands, decisively: speaking 'normally'*). How fascinating. So you've been a dozen times t'Sardinia?

ACKERMANN (*moronic howl*). Ohwa. Me? Did a spell at her Majesties . . .

PASCHKE*'s glare brings* ACKERMANN *to his senses.*

ACKERMANN. / Oh aye! 'Course a were! Nineteen times! Nineteen times I were on Sardinia. Y'gotta come one time. A tell yer. Lovely people them Sardines . . . And mega knockers . . .

PASCHKE (*cuts in*). Meself am happier down me allotment. Home's the best. I always say. Y'don't think so?

ACKERMANN. Aye. Oh aye. A say it too. Always. Home. Home is. Er. Home.

PASCHKE. X'zactly. We're on the same wave-length. / Do you know that film. 'Casablanca'? Your hat. Er. It really suits yer. / Er. It makes yer face. Y'know. Makes y'look dead hard.

ACKERMANN. Really? Well that's the only thing a mine what's hard like!

PASCHKE. And business? How's business?

ACKERMANN. Brilliant! Building up! Up n'up! We're into K.Y. Jelly now!

PASCHKE (*hisses*). Ackermann!

ACKERMANN. Mr t'you. Am still Mr Ackermann t'you.

Improvise the 'normal' conversation as they exit.

Scene Seven

Back at their gaff, they meander in, both dragging a few crappy balloons. ACKERMANN *has the Grannie bag. He tips its contents onto the floor.*

ACKERMANN. Two bags a bird-food. Six pink pampers. Incompetent!

PASCHKE. Incontinent y'twat.

ACKERMANN. Dentofix. And half a roll a *Rennies*. Y'want wun?

PASCHKE (*fiddling with the balloons*). Gob shut now! A mean it!

ACKERMANN. Pasch lad. Do you know what yer doing? / A mean. / Fair's fair. We that Grannie. Well a made a balls up there. But that's no reason t'go full bonkers! Do y'know what a nancy you look like? Brick-shit-house of bloke. Playing with a *Bugs Bunny* balloon! Man! The looks we got . . .

PASCHKE. Well a'd rather be normal too but . . .

ACKERMANN. Oh nice one! That does put me mind at rest!

PASCHKE. Take this.

ACKERMANN. What. And then y'take a photo of me? With that rabbit like. Nay! Mr Ackermann may be a berk. But that much of a berk!

PASCHKE. TAKE HOLD A THIS!!!

ACKERMANN. Give it here. / Right bunny boy? What now?

PASCHKE. Untie it! Carefully! Open it first. Hold the neck shut.

ACKERMANN. Like this?

PASCHKE (*nods*). Now stick it in yer gob. Breathe in deep. Hold it.

ACKERMANN. If it were Mona . . .

PASCHKE. Just do what a tell you t'do!!!

ACKERMANN *does it*.

PASCHKE. Good. Now say summat!

ACKERMANN (*Donald Duck voice*). What? What should a say? / Pasch! Me voice!!!

PASCHKE. Helium! Helium. Tint the same as air. Yer voice box takes to it completely different!

ACKERMANN (*Donald Duck voice*). If it stays like this. I shall bray you t'death with a shovel!

PASCHKE. / It'll be gone. Soon enough. / Now then. Wait. Am gonna call up Old Man Terre. You take another lung full a that Helium. 'Cuz we're gonna go up the scale a few notes. If y'get me meaning. It's gonna cost him! Price is up now! Under two-hundred-thousand we don't even get out a bed!

ACKERMANN (*Donald Duck*). Why me? (*Almost normal.*) Why me? (*Coughs.*) Bowha! Y'bloody heal'le'um. Din't half put the willies up me.

PASCHKE. They can't decode it! Get me? They can analyze yer voice t'bollocks! They'll never get it!

ACKERMANN. That dun matter because am not phoning up Old Man Terre. Not with that scare still stuck in me throat!

PASCHKE. Giv it 'ere!

> PASCHKE *dials, takes a deep drag.* TERRE *picks up the phone.*

TERRE (*snobby, arrogant*). Hello!?

PASCHKE (*helium-voiced*). That weren't very clever of yer.

TERRE. And to whom do I speak?

PASCHKE. Never mind that! If you wanna see yer son again. Then it costs double now. Two'undred. Very big ones. Do we understand each-other? . . . Otherwise . . .

TERRE (*laughs*). My 'son?' / Me. And Master Terre. 'see-each-other.' Do I want that? (*Laughs: and then hard.*) Now listen here. You can tell him I've put a stop on assorted credit cards. If he's 'skint' again. Then perhaps I've an opening for him as a cleaner. Perhaps.

PASCHKE. Yew dew know the seriousness of the situation. Yer son's in mortal danger! We could do anythin'.

TERRE. HE knows the seriousness of HIS situation. HIM! And anyway. My time is too expensive to be playing the sick games of a degenerate freak! In short. I don't know who you are. But my best advice is. Don't slave on that bloody pervert's band-wagon. Good day! (*Hangs up.*)

PASCHKE. Did you . . . did you hear that!?

ACKERMANN. He's a bloody swine.

PASCHKE. His OWN child!

ACKERMANN. And Yennifa and me. That we'd a miscarriage. When we so wanted . . .

> PASCHKE *dials again.*

ACKERMANN. What yer dewin now?

PASCHKE (*angry*). OUT OF ORDER. OUT OF ORDER!

> TERRE *picks up the phone.*

TERRE. Hello.

> *As soon as* PASCHKE *starts to speak* TERRE *hangs up.*

PASCHKE (*normal voice*). Now let me tell you! YOU BLOODY SWINE! This here's your child. YOUR SON! And he has his rights! Rights to be handled humanely. Everybody has the right . . . 'Cuz . . . 'cuz . . . everybody's summat very special! Even if they miss the bulls-eye! Everybody's summat highly special! Even life-guards are summat special! 'Specially life-guards. Just like you. You ought t'be ashamed a yerself. Carrying on like that. With yer own bloody kid! / To treat him like that. Y'listenin'? Y'simply don't do that! And NOW LISTEN T'ME. You'll say sorry. Right bloody now! Straight away! Are y' listening? STRAIGHT AWAY . . . Hello? Ah'looow!

ACKERMANN. He hung-up. Before you even said swine.

PASCHKE. He heard swine! He had t'hear that!

ACKERMANN. Yer right! WHAT NEEDS T'BE IS MEANT T'BE.

PASCHKE. Bloody moron!

ACKERMANN. X'zactly!

Scene Eight

TERRE *and* INA TERRE *at the dinner table, this time it's a fondu.*

INA TERRE. You could have called me!

TERRE. Darling. I did. But you were busy. Shaving your legs.

INA TERRE. I'm never too busy! Not when my son calls!

TERRE. How interesting. Should I call. There's nothing more 'pertinent' than you. Bent red-faced and panting slightly. A razor sliding over your shins. (*Turns the tray with the sauce dip.*) Please. Try the Caramel. It's a sonnet!

INA TERRE *tries it.*

TERRE. And?

INA TERRE. Interesting.

TERRE (*a little disappointed*). A little too dry. Such a conception.

INA TERRE. And he's alright? You say . . .

TERRE (*mouth full, indefinite*). Mmmm.

INA TERRE. And how do you like the wine?

TERRE (*tastes professionally*). Oh yes . . . perhaps a little . . . severe perhaps . . . (*Continues tasting.*) or . . .

INA TERRE. I've pissed in it.

TERRE. YOU'VE WHAT!

INA TERRE. Pinkled in it. It wasn't easy. I'd say. For the way you men are built. The wine bottle's more user-friendly.

TERRE (*decides to be amused*). Insatiable. Insatiable. You and your sexual fantasies.

INA TERRE. I knew it would arouse you.

TERRE (*laps it up*). Mmm. Ja'wohl!

INA TERRE. And he is? Ahem. Alright you say?

TERRE. Oh yes. With my Porsche under his bum he's not going sink immediately below the poverty line. Please. Could you turn the Caramel Dip to me . . .

INA TERRE. The Caramel's all gone.

TERRE. My little comfort-eater.

INA TERRE. And do I have good reason. I mean. You did say. He will be alright . . . or?

During the following, INA TERRE *affects little annoying mannerisms,* TERRE *corrects them and this disruption, to a certain extent, structures the monologue into an almost classical metre.*

TERRE. Pardon? / I *said*. 'He is as he always is.' Now let's not spoil the evening? You know!? I don't like to miss out our little rituals. These barely noticeable. Undervalued stigmata of daily routine. They're not only a pragmatic way of deciphering our complexes. No. Quite definitely they're also . . . pleasant. Leaving out of course. A certain originality of wit on the part of our midwife. In short. The style. The quality of our evening meal. IT'S OURS. Yours and mine. Our modest ritual. / Alongside the performance of our morning excretions. Our daily eighteen fifteen telephone chat. Me sitting to urinate. *Sensident* and *Colgate*. / Yes. The evening meal. Is truly the central feast of our bond. It's training for the senses. Enjoyment. AND. The practice of moderation. / A very pretty idea is coming to light. An intelligent cell culture. That has up to now. And through many centuries with almost undisturbed. And I do stress almost. Since I tend not to the beautification of reality. An intelligent cell culture. That has. Up to now. Made possible a practically complete turn around. And in the end. / I surrender nothing without a certain embarrassment. / This 'today I cook tomorrow you cook.' It has the light nuance of proletarian vulgarity about it. Somewhat similar to anal-intercourse. Don't you think so? I mean you do know. To scratch this ornamented column of our marriage. It wouldn't be very clever of us.

INA TERRE. I'm not hungry.

TERRE. You're quite intelligent. Educated. Within certain boundaries. What's the meaning of this raw formulation. 'I'm not hungry'?

INA TERRE. I'm not hungry. I don't like it.

TERRE. Please darling please. Don't allow your IQ to sink to the level of room temperature.

INA TERRE. Am leaving . . . (*Corrects herself.*) Am getting gone from yer.

TERRE (*thrilled*). Perfect! Per-fect. 'Am getting gone from yer.' A furrow formed of clay! The fields heavy with desire are given voice! Those desolate hammering stanzas have found language. You're brilliant. You see them. The last really worth saving . . . really dying. What am I saying!? Disappearing species. The human being. His beer in front of him. You even awaken the rip in the anorak. A 'LET ME TELL YEW SUMMAT' Sounding out! Yes! An overture evoking the wonderful world of women battered! Children abused! And all of it from clinically completely alcoholic men. Real ethics!? If anything has authenticity. Then that! And heavens if anything should be so distanced. So much another universe. So absolutely contrary to that. Then darling. WE ARE IT! (*He blows his nose, a little surprised by himself.*) 'J'aime çelà! Ces merveilleuses emotions que l'on subit sous le sevil de la pauvreté.' Darling. You make me sick. If your real concerns are for the lumpen proletariat. Do some charity work! And pass me the Remoulade.

INA TERRE. I will leave you.

TERRE (*just so*). Yes yes. If you could just . . . The Remoulade.

INA TERRE *stands and sticks her hand in the fondu.*

TERRE (*stops short, points at the fondu with a fork*). In God's name! Darling. That must be unbelievably painful.

INA TERRE (*sticks her other hand in*). You said it.

TERRE. An archaic act of self mutilation. Interesting. Only what does it prove? And to whom? You? Me?

INA TERRE. I hate you. I hate you. I hate you.

TERRE. Darling. You're hyperventilating! / Still. With all that clearly spoken redundancy. We should talk it over. But please. Do take your hands out of the fondu. They'll be done by now.

Blackout.

Scene Nine

PASCHKE *sprays air freshener and monologues the corpse.*

PASCHKE. Y'smell that? Cornflowers. It's made for freshening up yer toilet. But it's not so bad eh? / Definitely cornflowers. / We dint have enough for a new freezer. And since yer now on the turn. You gotta be sprayed a bit. / (*Deep breath.*) Oh man! Cornflowers! Does me heart in! Y'see. Well. / Well. A grew up on a farm. Not the world. Just a bit of a barn. Couple a pigs. A few rabbits. Poultry. Still. It wern't s'bad . . . Not that that interests you? No way! You and yer fat wallet! (*Angered.*) That's not everything! Y'understand me! (*Comes to his senses.*) My God! Now am running y'down too. Just like yer bloody shite you've got for a fa'ther. Bloody Nazi! . . . Aye well? Y'can ferget that. The shite and the Nazi. I mean he is yer fa'ther. A mean Bottom line. He is yer fa'ther. Eh? And you're his little lad. Just modern times in't it? You've t' hide it all these days. Not in fashion n'more. A Dad and his lad. Father n'son. Aye. A mean what my old man were. / Not that you've t'think he never thumped me. He did and hard and all. So hard a could have throttled him for it . . . Me Mum were always good for a cutlet. On my black eye a mean. 'It'll be better before yer twice married.' Her favourite line. / Lot a good that were. A never married once! Anyroad. It'll mend. That's the way things work. Eh? He kept me on the straight and narrow. Me old fella. And right he were and all. / What's odd is. It were only when he were sober. Drunk all he did were stroke me head. Problem were. Me Old Man. He were always . . . completely legless. . . . / (*Controls himself, quietly.*) Lad when a look at you. Well. Yer might well a been a heap a dogshit. Even found a (*Makes clear it's a pistol.*) shooter in yer jacket. But . . . halfways yer were just a naughty boy. With yer dimples n' . . . Did a lot a grinning. Eh? Lotta laffs? / Me tew. A'll tell yer. At your age. Man! What we did back then f'fun. (*Laughs.*) / (*Serious again.*) Just the way it comes. Just the way it bloody comes. 'No more Mr Nice Guy! Am here!' / Anyway. A've no fat wallet. But bad? Y'wouldn't a done so bad with me. And Ackers. He'd a made a good Mum . . . A mean. It weren't all roses for him. The way his Yennifa lost that kiddy. He could'a been dealt a better hand . . . Shite! A don't half run away at mouth. 'Til't bloody cows are long 'ome. Anyway. A wer only sayin'. It dint have ter be this way.

ACKERMANN (*outside the door*). Pash! Who you babbling with? (*Enters.*) Screw loose eh? Full bonkers.

PASCHKE. A've just sprayed our Thomas. He's gone a bit iffy!

ACKERMANN. Rees'n'bull. / Listen. A've got it! We've t'give 'em a sign'a life. Here. Newspaper. Polaroid camera. Got it off Big Dieter's lad. / (*Affectionate.*) Thomas? They call 'im Thomas?

PASCHKE. Mmmm.

ACKERMANN (*almost tender*). Thomas. / Bollocks anyway! We've got t'give 'em a sign of life. A paper. With the date on it. That'll give it a touch of professionalism.

PASCHKE. You've lost me Ackers!?

ACKERMANN. You've seen it on't telly! Put the hostage on a stool. Have look like he's re-heated vomit. And he says. 'Please do all you can! Get me out! They mean what they say!' And so on . . .

PASCHKE. Yeah. But for that we'll need a soddin' video.

ACKERMANN. Oh *we do* do we? Owt else? Do tell me 'cuz Big Dieter's lad's running a Cash'n'carry warehouse. Eh? Y'daft get. A chainsaw and a Polaroid and that's that!

PASCHKE. Ackers? Our Thomas is . . . dead.

ACKERMANN (*penny drops*). O yeah? Shite! (*Another penny drops.*) No problem. No fuckin' problem. It's better even. There'll be no sodding tricks. No secret signals as such.

ACKERMANN *tries to get the corpse on a chair.*

PASCHKE. Hey! Not s'rough there with our Thomas.

ACKERMANN. A wunt have t'be if you'd help me . . . Okay. x'zactly. Now . . . sit 'im./ S'watta yer reckon?

PASCHKE. Well? He's about as lively as you after a pint a pure voddy.

ACKERMANN. We gotta open his eyes. His eyes. And then you. You held his head up. From behind.

PASCHKE. Oh great! Then it's my mush that's all over't world on them artists impri'sessions.

ACKERMANN. Put an Aldi bag over yer head!

PASCHKE. Fair enough. But we're still flumoxed with his eyes.

ACKERMANN. Superglue! Or a bit a *Sella'tape*. Y'can't see nowt on them bloody *Polaroids* anyroad. We hang a bloody sign up front. 'We are serious! DEAD serious!' And then you stand behind. Lookin totally dangerous. / You could be IRA. You could be Lybian!

PASCHKE. A don't know her!? Lybbie Ann?

ACKERMANN. Gaddaffi's men y'bloody berk! A Lyb'E'ANN!

PASCHKE (*none the wiser*). Oh aye! Right! Sure. / Plastic bag on me head and a copy a today's 'Sun . . .!?'

ACKERMANN. Come on. Let's get on with it! Serious business, kidnapping!

PASCHKE. God, Ackers!? When you die science won't want yer liver. But they'll love yer brain. Never bin used.

ACKERMANN. Pasch!?

PASCHKE. Think about it man! Am I really gonna look like Public Enemy Number bloody Wun. An Aldi bag over me bloody once!

ACKERMANN. Just held a bread knife or summat?

PASCHKE (*shows the pistol*). A cud er . . .

ACKERMANN. Bloody 'ell Pasch. / Don't point that thing at me!?

PASCHKE. Found it in Thomas's pockets.

ACKERMANN. Mmmm? (*Chuffed.*) That Pasch. That is the G'spot! The multiple orgasm of our dangerousness!

Slapstick; the difficulty of getting TERRE *to look alive and at the same time, them, trying themselves to look dangerous.*

Scene Ten

PASCHKE *and* ACKERMANN *drinking, knackered.*

PASCHKE. 'RETURN T'SENDER!'

ACKERMANN. Mey be? Mey be if we'd have. Smeared a bit of *Heinz* on him.

PASCHKE. Simple as that. 'RETURN T'SENDER.'

ACKERMANN. Just on his cheek or something? Blood always looks gud.

PASCHKE. How can anyone be so heartless? Bloody heartless! A mean. Two hundred thousand's not bad price. Is it?

ACKERMANN. At least we've got a new freezer. Want another Looney Soup?

PASCHKE. *Tennants* and Thommy on the same shelf. / Puts me off.

ACKERMANN. Do yer or don't yer?

PASCHKE. Oh. Get us one.

ACKERMANN. We're gonna have t'bury him. Thomas. It is his rights.

PASCHKE. And I'll say a few words. Has t'be a few words.

ACKERMANN. What? What'll y'say?

PASCHKE. Dunno. A'll tell him that he were done in by two zeros. And that we're the last a the famous twats!

ACKERMANN. When my time comes. Promise me. A won't be sent off by the likes a us. Eh? / Got any fags?

PASCHKE. No.

ACKERMANN. You can have Mona t'nite. You can do her up. Right nice. A few candles and Bob's yer Uncle . . .

PASCHKE. There should be some in me jacket.

ACKERMANN *searches, comes back.*

ACKERMANN (*crushes a packet*). Empty. / And 'er. There in't no breath in Mona either. Not n'more.

PASCHKE. Morbid.

ACKERMANN. Fabric fatigue. Everything has its 'best by' date. (*Stupid.*) But a 'filled up' life . . . the lass lived it.

PASCHKE. When Thomas is six foot under. We'll sell off the wreaths. You can get yerself a new Mona.

ACKERMANN. Oh aye. We'll live in passion. 'Til us days end. / What would you have done with it? The loot?

PASCHKE (*too much for him*). Well a? . . . Yeah . . . ah. And you?

ACKERMANN. A would'a bought me Yennifa back.

PASCHKE. Ah? A financial arrangement?

ACKERMANN. No I a . . .

PASCHKE. Did you a . . .

ACKERMANN. Ja'make'her? No she . . .

PASCHKE. Did JA'MAY'KA? No she always 'came' without always 'came' without me asking! me asking!

PASCHKE. / Tint love that though? Is it? Eh?

ACKERMANN. Who's bothered about that bollocks? She were always well pumped up!

Both laugh.

Scene Eleven

ACKERMANN, *back to us, pisses.* PASCHKE *strenuously digs. They're in the process of burying* TERRE *on a tip.*

PASCHKE. Ackers! There's a time and a place! This is a burial and not a bog.

ACKERMANN. So? I ought'a draw it up n'spit it owt? If y'gotta go y'gotta go. The Law a Nature Pasch. Can't do nowt abowt it. / Look. A Teddy? x'cept he's got no head . . . but it can't be far off. Can . . . got it! / On it goes and. And. 'Cadabra!

PASCHKE. A bloody teddy. Is not a headstone! Find summat else.

ACKERMANN (*the Teddy*). Times have changed. Eh? It dint kick it from bein' stroked t'much. Look. Stabbed. Cut open from his back to his bum. Oh tell yer Pasch. With this 'new generation' Godknows what's on its way fer us . . .

PASCHKE. Don't come it Ackers. You blew up frogs. Jumped on cats' heads!

ACKERMANN. Shit! Hey! A toaster! Still in its box! Guarantee an' all!

PASCHKE. A toaster. Has got t'be. The most stupidest thing imaginable for a bloody headstone.

ACKERMANN. The toaster's for us Pasch!

PASCHKE. Guarantee and all?

ACKERMANN. Cracking!

PASCHKE. Pack it up. And let's get on with . . . the rest of the . . . arrangements.

ACKERMANN *searches*. PASCHKE *digs, suddenly he screams.*

ACKERMANN (*'holding his heart'*). God! What yer bloody ballin' at!?

PASCHKE. 'Ere . . . 'Ere . . . 'Ere.

ACKERMANN (*at the grave*). What? / That can't be a . . .

PASCHKE. Have we?

ACKERMANN. Looks like it.

PASCHKE. Shall a dig somewhere else?

ACKERMANN. What? Ney? So we dig up another? Ney! Two's two too many! Will just stick our Thomas in with it. He won't be so alone.

PASCHKE. / Seems like it's bin a while 'ere. Means our Thomas'll have a guide. For the here-after like.

ACKERMANN. You believe in that? Life after death?

PASCHKE. Dunno? Yew?

ACKERMANN. / Like tew. Do bailiffs get into heaven?

PASCHKE. Could be.

ACKERMANN. And that bat from the dole.

PASCHKE. Mumm. / Maybe you get reborn as summat else.

ACKERMANN. That bat from the dole ought'a be a frog. Then a cud . . .

PASCHKE. Ackers!!! Leave out the glory distails. / And what would you come back as?

ACKERMANN. / Maybe a President or summat.

PASCHKE. You with yer dirty fingernails?

ACKERMANN. Well? Summat completely dif'rent. A 'Ladyshave.' Y'know. The razor for the legs. The armpits. (*Laughs.*) And the 'specially sensitive 'Bikini Bits!'

PASCHKE. A 'Ladyshave' in't alive.

ACKERMANN. Buzzes dunt it? What's life Pasch? Owt what scoffs shits and more or less thinks shit? (*Laughs.*) When a were little me Mum were always wannin' t'know what a wanned t'be. 'Astronaut!' A always said. And me Mum. 'That you will be my lad!' That were me Mum! 'If yer really want it. Y'get it.' And me Dad always said she shouldn't start on't booze before mid-day.

PASCHKE. Me. I dig. And you philosophise! Life lad. Let me tell you. Is the best there is.

ACKERMANN. So y'say. Up to yer neck in the carcasses of two TV's. Empty bottles of long boozed bargin spirits. And 'jam rags.' / And er. What would sir like t'be brought back as? A Pasch? THREW N'THREW? Mr Paschke. Eh?

PASCHKE. Well just so as you know. A poet.

ACKERMANN. A poet!? Say that in public and you'll put everybody t'sleep! / (*Suddenly distracted.*) There. Look. An old coffee grinder!

PASCHKE. Where?

ACKERMANN. Might still work! / There! There! / Be our luck! 'Specially now they've cut us 'leccie off. On account a your shite investment in Thomas.

PASCHKE. No way am puttin me hands on that.

ACKERMANN. But yer want yer coffee?

PASCHKE. In't middle 'ert ribs?

ACKERMANN. Freshly ground! Smell it Pasch!

PASCHKE. Alright. But am not gonna look! No way! No looking! A'll grab it. An you get it cleaned.

ACKERMANN. Give it here.

PASCHKE, *face screwed, fishes the grinder from the corpse and passes it to* ACKERMANN.

PASCHKE. And you reckon it runs?

ACKERMANN. Like a greyhound!

PASCHKE *feels sick and chokes.* ACKERMANN *packs away the grinder.*

ACKERMANN. In its own time like. This funeral's turning into a good earner! Anyway. Mr Poet?

PASCHKE. It wer only a . . . may be a'll be er . . . Er.

ACKERMANN. You'll be a what? At the end of it all? A fly on shite?

PASCHKE (*thinks*). / Ahw. It's all bollocks anyway! If you're gunna be a 'Ladyshave.' Then . . . then . . . a'll be yer battery. Wunna them long life rechargeables!

ACKERMANN (*laughs*). Nice one! Ace Pasch! The both of us. Trimming my Yennifa's hole. We'll be the best buy there is! Quality! The Marks n' Sparks of secondary sexual hair depletion! / Din't expect that. Did yer? Very educational my literature!

PASCHKE. Oh yeah yeah. / We'll b'fine . . . (*He sees something. Holds back.*) There. There! That's it! Thatsit!

ACKERMANN (*follows* PASHCKE's *stare*). A can see nowt but a fat duck. And that's headless tew!

PASCHKE. That's not a duck Ackers! It's a Cherub. An' angel! Every respectable grave demands the likes of that!

ACKERMANN. / Dunno? / Can't say I'd want an headless starkers lady-gnome over me. Look at that fat arse! A mean. Without an head. Not that a woman has to have an head fer me to have a good time with her. / But the arse on it. The arse . . .

PASCHKE. You've no notion of undertaking. Undertaking is not about the arse. But the soul. The soul is the heavenly part of us. That bit of us with which our spirit does its heavenly rejoicing. / Find that Teddy's head. And we can get started!

ACKERMANN. Rejoicing?

PASCHKE. Rejoicing!

ACKERMANN. Yes! In heaven we will rejoice . . .?

PASCHKE. Twenny four hours a day! Find that head.

ACKERMANN searches, PASCHKE shovels.

ACKERMANN. Gorrit! It more a rabbit's head. But it'll do!

PASCHKE. Rabbit's grand! Suits Tommy. Oh aye. And er. Tommy's companion here. It's more a Tommysina. A've got her dug free now. She's got a kinda skirt on. Slips threw the fingers like a strawberry coated 'Durex.'

ACKERMANN. Latex! Thomas'll have his fun there!

PASCHKE. Are we gunna do her a headstone?

ACKERMANN. Yennifa.

PASCHKE. Ackers!? Kiss me bloody arse with y'bloody Yennifa! (*Into the grave.*) I christen thee. Edith. Edith Stock'losa.

ACKERMANN (*attentive*). Woah! Yeh Pasch! The heavenly Soulman. With a hell of a hard-on!!

PASCHKE (*wild*). Y'leave that! Y'leave that! Y'just leave that!

ACKERMANN. Awrite. Wer only a remark! Nice name though . . . Edith.

PASCHKE (*threatening*). LEAVE IT! Bloody Pauper! The likes a you dunt take my Edith's name in their gob!!!

ACKERMANN. The likes a . . .?

PASCHKE. Spit it out. Now. Right away!

ACKERMANN. 'Am no bloody Pauper!?'

PASCHKE. The likes of Edith . . .

ACKERMANN. . . . Who's a bloody Pauper!?

PASCHKE. Am not having her dragged through the muck.

ACKERMANN. You poxy little fucking looser. Still playin' the big I am. An' yer nowt! Nowt wi'owt me. Here. (*Shows his thumb.*) The muck under my nail. That's what you are without me! A've only t'mention it! Christmas! Before last. Who were the bugger what cried his eyes out? Who? 'Cuz there were no other bugger that give a bugger all about him? And who deprived me a'my Mona? Who? YOU. Y'gobshite!

PASCHKE. Bollocks! Nowt like it Mr Ackermann! Nowt like it! I saved you! Sleeping on a park bench. We nowt more than a 'Telegraph and Argus' for a blanket. Cunt even look after yer own pully. HELPLESS! That's what you were. Mr Ackermann. It were me what took you in! In all yer HELPLESSNESS. Put a roof over yer head. Got y'back on yer feet. That's my nature!

ACKERMANN. On me feet? Am a coalman! A tramp 'em raw f'two fifty n'hour!

PASCHKE. And a fine wage fer a man with your intellectual capacities.

ACKERMANN. Aye! And what you've got between yer legs is a 'fine' give-away for the contents a yer brain-box. Chlorine-cock!

PASCHKE. Oh! So y'reckon the Oak is pissed off. 'Cuz the wild pig pisses on it?

ACKERMANN.?

PASCHKE. A tell y'summat fer nowt . . .

ACKERMANN. SHUT IT! You remember how those lads roughed yer up. Deutschland über alles and the like! Me! I went looking for 'em! My god. A'knifed their tyres. A shudda blackened yer eyes!

PASCHKE. 'Cuz yerself. Yer a little Hitler . . .

ACKERMANN. Oh? and if that's . . .

PASCHKE. . . . ADOLF ACKERMANN . . .

ACKERMANN. . . . yer Stalin. JOSEPH PASCHKE!

> PASCHKE *and* ACKERMANN *fight. Choreograph: a silent-movie without music. They expose all the repressed hatred in their relationship - brought into being through external poverty and need. The fight is disciplined, only minimal 'dirty tricks.' It ends suddenly. They recover themselves, assist each other as they do.*

ACKERMANN. Now we're bashing each other's brains in!?

PASCHKE. Aye. And how does a herd a wild ponies deal with a wolf? Put their heads together and kick outward. Out towards the world! / (*He puts down the Teddy torso near the grave, next to the rabbit skull.*) We do the exact opposite!

ACKERMANN. Maybe we aren't the same. Humans! Eh Pasch? That offal like us waz 'evolutioned' from a different sorta ape. Like a, like. Genetically say. Related. The ape what thought a Lion were a bed-spread!

PASCHKE. Bollocks! Do up yer neck button. We'll give Tommy his last rites. Words he never heard while he were still breathing.

Short pause as they stand at the grave.

PASCHKE. Ower Father. Who art in heaven . . .

ACKERMANN. . . . oh tah very much! For what we're abowt t'scoff. And scoff along with us God if yer like!

PASCHKE *glares at* ACKERMANN.

ACKERMANN. / Sorry! A just dint eat owt decent since this morning. Don't y'think a minute's silence would do okay?

PASCHKE. / Aye. Right. The likes of US. We can't see the likes of HIM on his way . . . Start it up! A've got no second hand!

ACKERMANN. Now! Mine. Yer Royal Pashness. Has an autostop. We peeps!

PASCHKE. Off y'go!

ACKERMANN. Ah 'ttention! On yer marks. / Set. / Go!

PASCHKE *and* ACKERMANN *heads bowed, hands over their balls; a football free kick wall of two. After a while* ACKERMANN *yawns,* PASCHKE *brings him around with a glare. The peeps goes, it's a banal melody.*

Scene Twelve

The TERRES. *He's prepared fish. Embarrassingly inappropriate for her . . . With her bandaged hands, she tries desperately to fillet the fish.*

TERRE. Oh darling. Just say the word. I help you manage that. After all, that's why one is here.

He doesn't fillet it himself, rather he pushes the cutlery into her wounded hands and slices, leading her as if he was teaching a child. She tenses with pain but holds still.

TERRE. So. A little cut. Lift lightly. And hey presto! Beautiful fillets . . .

INA TERRE. Why fish?

TERRE. Pike-perch darling. Pike perch.

INA TERRE. Why!!? I shouldn't . . . My hands. They'll scar . . .

TERRE (*friendly laugh*). And you think . . . that then . . . I'd love you less. (*Kisses her.*) . . . And now. For the sake of Old Lang Synne. Turn Herr Pike-Perch over. And! 'Voilà.'

INA TERRE *shivers with pain.* TERRE *sits again at his place.*

TERRE. A toast! A toast to your not unheard 'cry for help.' A toast to your recovery!

INA TERRE. Did he telephone?

TERRE. Who?

INA TERRE. Thomas. Did he telephone again?

TERRE. Oh yes! And he said hello. He's doing well. Has an exam soon. Dodged the questions a little . . . But I suspect it will lead to a promotion.

INA TERRE (*almost crying*). Promotion? / He's hooked! Injecting again?

INA TERRE. Of course not darling. Of course not. Empty your glass. You'll be the image of your son. An office party in its end phase.

INA TERRE drinks, uncertain. The glass in both her bandaged hands.

TERRE. And now look how beautifully you do that. With those terrible terrible cat paws ... Although ... (*Laughs.*) ... it's not without its own certain comedy.

He mimics her and laughs. She laughs along with him, tiredly.

INA TERRE. And?

TERRE. You mean?

INA TERRE. Will he study again?

TERRE. Holidays first. Jamaica. Then Harvard. Philosophy of Law.

INA TERRE (*confused, happy*). Philosophy. / Then it is you he takes after?

TERRE. Never in doubt as far as I was concerned.

INA TERRE. And?

TERRE (*a little hectic*). And . . . And he's now driving a Mini Traveller. Built some time in the Neolithic. But . . .

INA TERRE. Did you transfer him money? Just a start.

TERRE. No. He didn't want it.

INA TERRE (*disbelief*). He didn't want . . .

TERRE (*a false laugh*). Exactly! Exactly that must have been the expression on my face. He got me at the department. Said. 'Thanks Papa. But I have to make my way without you.' and then he hung up. I was there with a few colleagues. 'My good God' said my assistant. 'He must have captured the Yeti.' The Yeti! (*Laughs coldly.*) Imagine that!

INA TERRE (*happier*). The Yeti. (*Laughs a little hysterically.*) / You've hardly touched it.

TERRE (*brash*). Because I. (*Fills her mouth.*) Thomas and I . . . I mean . . . is it everyday that one can be so happy? . . . I.

He laughs, food sprays from his mouth. He's embarrassed and puts a serviette to his mouth.

INA TERRE (*laughs warmly*). On the vase.

TERRE (*jumps up and wipes it away, gipping as he does*). I . . . I've the manners of a . . . garden hose. I am sorry. I . . . I . . . Did I . . . hit you? I mean . . . Excuse me. It must be quite grotesque for you. But . . .

INA TERRE. Yes.

TERRE. How do you mean?

INA TERRE (*calm*). Yes. Quite grotesque.

TERRE. You mean I . . .

INA TERRE. You're lying! You don't know anything about him!

TERRE. And how do come to this conclusion? / Of course I . . .

INA TERRE (*bawls*). Stop it! JUST STOP IT!

He's stunned to silence, afraid. A short pause.

INA TERRE (*not looking at him*). Now you're going to cry aren't you? You've got your Mediterranean goggle-eyes in again? All slimy at the corners. No doubt you're stroking your lip to calm yourself. And now you'll lean forward. Think about going on the offensive? But not with your under-arm on your knee. And rocking like a baby. (*Looks at him.*) I'd like an answer. Spit it out! YOU WET FART!

TERRE (*defeated*). Ina. I did look for him. Really. I . . . started a search for him. I . . . I couldn't know. I . . .

INA TERRE *lights a cigarette. She goes to him, slowly. He backs away. Momentarily it seems she might hit him. He's not worth it. She gives him the cigarette.*

TERRE. But I . . . But I don't smoke.

INA TERRE (*looks at the fish*). And so you shouldn't.

TERRE. Nooh. Not that!

INA TERRE. Do it!

TERRE. Ina. I . . .

INA TERRE. Do it I said!!!

Sickened and shaking TERRE *stubs out the cigarette in the fish. As* INA TERRE *begins her exit,* TERRE *sits, horrified.*

TERRE (*soundlessly*). I'm sorry.

INA TERRE (*at the door*). You will be sorry! Should I NOT find him!

Scene Thirteen

Back at the gaff, with the corpse, PASCHKE *couldn't do it.*

ACKERMANN. That you Pash! That yer such a soft bloody sod. A cream egg! / When GOD above finally does do summat. It'll be dragging you. As a stiff. From the tip! / If you don't get bloody sharp sharpish. Then little Tommy here. He'll out-live us.

PASCHKE (*serious, quotes or reads*). 'As we see it. Neither the literary 'qualities'. Nor the almost arbitrary relating of worthless everyday personal gossip . . .'

ACKERMANN. . . . Wat yer on abowt? . . .

PASCHKE. '. . . Has any possibility of being accommodated in our publications portfolio.'

ACKERMANN. Y'sounding like a bailiff!

PASCHKE. Me diary! A sent it to a publisher. 'Arbitrary worthless everyday personal gossip.' A put me everything into it. EVERYTHING! All what a done. Do do . . . and. Aye. Well. A flashed it up a bit. But mainly the facts as they are.

ACKERMANN. Pasch the poet! Am gob'smacked! / What yer call it then? Y'bloody book? 'Horst Paschke. Life with Chlorinated Water.'

PASCHKE. Y'dick'ead. A did what writers do. Give meself a pseudonym.

ACKERMANN. Oh a silly name?

PASCHKE (*embarrassed*). Lay off. Let it be. Bollocks anyroads. / With the ransom. / With the booty! I would'a launched it meself. Right flash. 'Rinaldo Manzini . . . '

ACKERMANN (*bawls with joy*). . . . . Rinaldo Manzini? . . .

PASCHKE. '. . . A Lifetime of Suffering . . .'

ACKERMANN. . . . Our Pasch calls himself after a Pizza!

PASCHKE. You brownholer! It's a name what . . . SINGS!

ACKERMANN. Oh aye! Big time! Rinaldolini. Big time.

PASCHKE. Anyway! Am nowt 'arbitrary.' I've bin cicum'sized!

ACKERMANN. Bobbies' helmet boy! I've shiftin' kidneys. That dunt make me owt special!

PASCHKE. And yer fingerprints? / Think on Ackers. Tint any others like 'em in the whole wide world!

ACKERMANN (*looks at his finger*). Okay. Right. But! With all that coal muck . . . What's mine say? 'Schneider Coal an' Combustibles (Ltd.) El Tee Dee.' Y'd have t'give it a hell of a good scrub t'see half a difference. And even then bung on some a yer chlorine . . . A dunt. A dunno . . . / Ney. No way Pasch. Don't make me special. Pope. Mass murderer. / That's special.

PASCHKE. Start at the start lad. What were it yer Yennifa always said? 'There must a been summat to him.' Ower pauper Ackers.

ACKERMANN. And yours? . . . Yewer Edith?

PASCHKE (*dreamily*). That a'd 'me own special smile.' So me EE'dee sed. 'Summat warm shone owt of me. Summat brownish with stars in.' So she sed. Like a cow we sparks . . .

ACKERMANN. Mmm? / Do it then!

PASCHKE *attempts his special smile.* ACKERMANN *watches sceptically, gets closer.*

ACKERMANN. Summat brown y'say?

PASCHKE. Mmm.

ACKERMANN. Well in the middle yer red. At rim brown. But stars . . .? A don't see stars.

PASCHKE. Y'BLOOY WELL WILL DO! 'Rudimentation.' If there's summat y'dunt use n'more. Then it. Now listen t'this. It. D'E'volves . . . Yer webbed toes. Yer brain. Or yer tail like.

ACKERMANN. Hold on Pasch! There's nowt 'D'E'volved' about my tail!

PASCHKE. Ackers! Yer tails at the back of yer!? / Yer could call it yer bush? / The extension of yer Ver'ta'bra!

ACKERMANN. You calling me a trans-sister!? A've no bloody bush. / (*Thinks.*) And when you pull that mush. Y'glow up again?

PASCHKE. X'zactly. / But then what have I got t'smile abowt? Nowt against you Ackers but. Well you're more for me digestion.

ACKERMANN (*thoughtfully*). Oh yeah . . . (*Concludes.*) Yennifa thort it were great! That a cud pump a song out a me arm-pit. 'On't Ilkley Moor baht tat.' 'Specially in't summer. Cuz a me sweat. (*Sticks his hand in his arm-pit and demonstrates. Sees* PASCHKE*'s screwed up face.*) Not bad eh? Quite a rude-e-instrumentation. (PASCHKE *nods.*) Aye . . . well . . . er . . . a reckon . . . YES! Got it! / Whatever Yennifa were. She fownd me 'specially special. When a got her on her belly. A'd stroke her like. She were a carthorse of a woman. A'd stroke her from her neck down tew 'er bum. 'Nub'dey else in the whole world can do that as long as yew do.' So she always said.

PASCHKE. See!

ACKERMANN. Sod me speciality! A wer up fer a fuck! She wanned t'be stroked! And on top-a-that. A were allergic to her nightcream. A'd paws on me like a Ba'boon.

PASCHKE. She seemed t'like yer tenderness.

ACKERMANN (*laughs friendly; again thoughtful, and - tuts*). Part a my unique bloody strokin' finger-printin' played n'bloody part.

PASCHKE. She seemed t'want it.

ACKERMANN. Then why didn't she just quietly turn on her back. And shut her gob abowt jam'rags. Her periods went on fer twenny'eight days a month. Anyroad. She went off with a gyno'cologist.

PASCHKE. / My gyno'cologist. / The wun my EE'dee buggered off with. / E wer a poet. E gave my EE'dee poetic dedications. T'forget me. And she did. And all that after a'd built her a fantastic imitation stone fireplace in us bungalow! Flames better than real'ens. A solved the problem we a video! Put in a TV with a tape of a fire in it. A TELL YER. Crackled n'spat like middle of a country n'western number.

PASCHKE *sings 'Country Roads Take Me Home.'* ACKERMANN *gets excited and sings along a bit. A short sad pause.*

ACKERMANN. Women are pretty stupid.

PASCHKE (*sad*). She were lying there she were. With her poet darling. On the imitation fur rug. Doing him a gob job as I come in.

ACKERMANN. Shite!

PASCHKE. Ackers. A reckon the both of us. We're too bloody stupid fer women.

ACKERMANN. Mmm? / Hey! A know now! What a wanna be like. In me born again life. Not a president. Or a 'Ladyshave.' But as poet-gyno'cologist. That would have all angles covered.

PASCHKE. Aye. Can't fault it. And t'that . . . Cheers.

ACKERMANN. Y'just gotta think about. It's like am always telling yer. A bit of imagination. / (*Returns the toast.*) Neck it Pasch.

Suddenly a bright light blasts through the window.

MEGAPHONE. Mr Paschke! Horst! This is Special Patrol Group regional commander speaking. We know you've taken Mr Thomas Terre hostage. Know that he's quite probably in there with you now. My officers have secured all exits. All entrances. Stairwell. Roof. Your situation is already hopeless. Please. Don't make it worse by acting in an ill-considered manner! / (*Not a direct threat, just assumed and secure of his power.*) In the next ten minutes. That's . . . (*A time.*) . . . you will leave the building with your hands held high. Clearly visible. If you ignore my wishes. My only alternative will be to issue my officers with an order. 'Do whatever's necessary to liberate the hostage.' Should you wish to make contact with me. Then do so at the following number. Seven one. Three three. Zero three. I repeat . . .

During the above ACKERMANN *hectically puts out the lights and then drags* PASCHKE, *who through it all simply sat there apathetically, with him under the table.*

ACKERMANN. What now? Get-away car? Pilot n'plane? Central America?

PASCHKE (*chuckles crazily*). Your situation is hopeless.

ACKERMANN. What?

PASCHKE. Hopeless. Hopeless. Hopeless. Worthless everyday personal gossip. Dunt fit in the programme.

ACKERMANN. Oh fuckin' hell! Cunt you chooze a better time t'go do'fuckin'lalee. (*Tugs up the phone, dials.*) Cop on ter this! Mr Commander! A've a cannon here! And a'll blow young Tommy's bloody brains out! Aye! Him first. Then me! / Sod yer 'hands held high.' And now. Get this. In half an hour. There's a fully tanked Porsche outside our door. And am talking PORSCHO TURBO! There's a suitcase in the boot. With two hundred thousand portraits of her majesty! In well used and abused denominations. Are yer with me so far? Good! Now the airport! There's a birdie there fer us. An it's to be blast-off ready. That's starters! Y'with me? And if yer try any tricks. Y'might as well have the body bag out! (*Hangs up, he's chuffed.*) How were that!? Cool or what!? Bruce Willis can kiss my (*Pats his*

arse.) Demme Moore / Er? Pasch? (*Smells his hand.*) A
think a might a shit meself . . .

Telephone rings. PASCHKE *picks it up. He gives it to*
ACKERMANN.

ACKERMANN. What now!? Trouble with the Porsche? /
Yennifa? (PASCHKE *begins to laugh.*) Tone? What tone? /
Have I someone else? / No course I am. Chuffed t'bits that
you. / It's just . . . Right now like. I can't like now . . .
What? / Guess wat? / Not now. Not now . . . / Okay. You
thought about it and . . . Just listen. It's a bad time right
now . . . / Back? T'me!? / No. Course. Chuffed. Big time.
Big time chuffed. / Me? Am alone. / Listen luv. A really
can't . . . / What d'yer mean called? What? Ooow? . . . A've
got t'go . . . Yennifa! . . . / What's the cunt's called? There
in't no-one. / (*Angry.*) How do you know? / Si'mona. That's
her name. / Simona! . . . Yeah! A call 'er 'Mona.' Kiss my
arse! (*Hangs up, crumples.*)

PASCHKE. A lifetime's suffering.

ACKERMANN. Gob shut!

MEGAPHONE. Mr Paschke. We're prepared to fulfil your
demands. However you must convince us. That your
hostage is still alive. Let Mr Thomas Terre come to the
kitchen window.

ACKERMANN. Shit. Shit! SHIIIIT!

PASCHKE (*suddenly calm*). We both put Aldi carriers over
us heads. Look out the window. Then they can't know
who's who?

*PASCHKE gets the bags. They pull them over their heads,
tear in eye-holes and go to the window.*

ACKERMANN. Don't always be poking me head! Yer finger!

PASCHKE. Tint a finger Pasch. Definitely not a finger!

ACKERMANN & PASCHKE *go back to the telephone.*

PASCHKE (*into the phone*). So a hope it's clear now . . . You
heard us. Half an hour . . . / Then never mind a Porsche.
A Jag'll do.

ACKERMANN. A Jag. Pasch!? This in't James Bond!

PASCHKE (*phone*). Thinking about it. It's Porsche or nowt . . . half an hour a said . . . Yeah. And a question . . . / Kiss me arse! / A just wanna ask a question. / Truth now. Or all hell breaks loose here! Right. What d'yer think t'the name. Rinaldo Manzini? . . . / Why? Just a simple question! (*Listens and hangs up angrily.*)

ACKERMANN. What did he say?

PASCHKE. Wanned t'know if a wanned summat t'eat. A pizza!

ACKERMANN. / Pasch?

PASCHKE. Yeah?

ACKERMANN. Horst. A don't think am really the Bruce Willis type. Am' brickin' in me boots.

PASCHKE. / You can go.

ACKERMANN. Yer not . . . annoyed?

PASCHKE. Nooh . . . Ackers. A got yew inter this. Just tell 'em a threatened yer.

ACKERMANN. Yer a great bloke Horst.

PASCHKE. You tew Lothar.

ACKERMANN. Right . . . well . . . better get off then.

PASCHKE. Aye. Off y'go. That we Yennifa. You'll put that right. 'Better before yer twice married.'

ACKERMANN. When yer inside. We'll visit yer. Beer n'cakes an' owt yer want. You'll be a fat happy pig in shit.

PASCHKE. That's nice a you an'Yennifa . . .

ACKERMANN. And as soon as yer out. Holidays! Bloody Jamaica! Ja . . .

PASCHKE. . . . make her?

ACKERMANN. No she cum of she come of her own accord.

PASCHKE *laughs.*

ACKERMANN. Aye. And a think she did and all. This time anyway. / Alright. See thee later Pasch!

PASCHKE. Aye. See thee later Ackers.

> ACKERMANN *goes slowly to the door. Turns back the once. And then off he charges.* PASCHKE *gets on the table.*

PASCHKE. HERE IS HORST PASCHKE! MR HORST PASCHKE! Never seen that before. Eh? Not in yer rule book. Yer got me in yer sights. But I've me in me sights! A reckon you've missed the bulls-eye. Eh? / Yer know what? Now you've got t'liberate me from meself. MY DAY'S COME! Mr Horst Paschke the HOSTAGE has t'be liberated from Horst Paschke the HOSTAGE-TAKER. That's how it works in a free country! / Take a look at the way so'ciety as an whole. How it goes abowt with hostages. Shows yer what worth. Society as an whole. What worth it pits on human beings. / Horst Paschke is now a hostage. Horst Paschke. Citizen. Life guard. Has a right to be saved from the bandit. Horst Paschke! Is that clear . . .
(PASCHKE *begins to sing the German National Anthem.*)

A volley 'salutes' him. He crashes onto the table, crumples in the fetal position.

Scene Fourteen

TERRE *and* INA TERRE, *both in black before their laid-out son. Her hands are no longer bandaged but they still look bad.*

TERRE. Oh Darling. I couldn't know . . . (*Cries and then angry.*) A maniac. Mentally disturbed pig. They should have gassed the swine! Gassed him!

INA TERRE. Yes.

TERRE. And I was always so . . . so cruel . . . cruel to him. Our Thomas.

INA TERRE. Yes.

TERRE. And to you . . . to you too.

INA TERRE. Yes.

TERRE. Can you forgive me?

INA TERRE. Kiss my . . . (*On second thoughts don't.*)

TERRE. And I forgive you. I forgive you too. Why's it always so. That the worst must happen before you . . .

INA TERRE (*bullets out a laugh*). The happy end? / Without that it's meaningless. / (*Tired.*) We'll begin again.

TERRE. And . . . Your hands . . .

INA TERRE. A transplant from my arse.

TERRE. You shouldn't say such things.

INA TERRE. Why? / I'd like to know why. Why he smells like. Cornflowers.

TERRE. Cornflowers? (*Sniffs.*) Now that you say so. Really! But cornflowers? / No. It's more. / Excuse me. How can I say it. / More like a public toilet.

INA TERRE. Cornflowers!

TERRE. Of course. As you wish.

INA TERRE. / I feel . . .

TERRE. Fear. Rage. Sadness. An unbelievable emptiness. A sort of oscillating condition of irreversible loss of the senses. / Darling. I feel exactly the same way.

INA TERRE. I feel . . .

TERRE. Don't say it. Don't torture yourself.

INA TERRE. I feel . . . Slightly . . . Peckish . . . Fillet of venison in red-wine sauce. With a full bodied 'Villages.' Exactly. / I feel a gentle pregnancy of appetite.

TERRE. / You feel!!?

   INA TERRE *nods.*

TERRE. / I know a very good restaurant. You'll like it. Oh I do love you Ina.

INA TERRE. Don't threaten me!

TERRE. I'll order us a taxi.

INA TERRE. I want to adopt a starving child. One of those with flies in its eyes.

TERRE. Of course of course. After the meal. Okay?

They exit like an old married couple. She rests her head on his shoulder and a hand on his hip. He marches off, flagging down a cab. She stands there.

A lonely and terrible cry . . .

ACKERMANN. P–A–S–C–H!!!

Curtain.

MALARIA

by Simone Schneider

translated by Penny Black

'Who is at the gate?'
Euripides, *The Bacchae*

Simone Schneider was born in Duisberg in 1962 and grew up in Niederrhein. She worked as a journalist and began writing for the theatre in 1989. Her plays include: *Die National-galeristen, Drei Bilder* (1994), *Orwell, ein Stück* (1996), *Malaria* which had its premiere at the Hamburg Schauspielhaus in March 1998, *Ägypte*r (1999) and *Kameliendame* (2000). She has also written award-winning plays for radio.

Malaria was first performed in English as a rehearsed reading in the *New German Voices* season in the Theatre Upstairs on 5 December 1997 with the following cast:

DIONYSOS	Chris Gascoyne
KETTLING	Nicholas LePrevost
ISA	Jodhi May
MICHEL	Patrick O'Kane
LISA	Maggie Steed

Director Rufus Norris
Translator Penny Black

Characters

KETTLING, *an investor*
ISA, *his daughter*
MANIA, *unemployed*
MICHEL, *her boyfriend, unemployed*
DIONYSOS
LISA, *his mother*
GOD'S FIGHTER

Setting

Germany, the depression
A square
A stairwell in East Berlin

The First Night

Floodlight. The square is a building site. ISA *is standing on a footplank resting on the ground. She is in a short suit and has blonde curls, à la Schiffer, and a pistol in her hand. She aims at a rum bottle.* DIONYSOS *enters. He's wearing a woman's dark-coloured fur coat, has black curls and a guitar under his arm.* ISA *slides the pistol into her bag. He walks past her. She speaks to him.* DIONYSOS *stops.*

ISA. Sitting on a building site in the middle of the night is really great. There's a feeling of actually being somewhere. Nothing's quite right, the world's full of corners and edges. Mad, as if it's been all churned up. I'm Isa. Not from round here. Don't know anyone in this city. Do you speak? Only if you're drunk?

She passes him the bottle.

That's not milk, baby.

She sits down on the ground and drinks.

My girlfriend phoned at six. It rings, I pick up and straightaway: the long distance phone call thing! You know, that peculiar gap between you and the universe. How's things? Bea asked. She was two classes above me and is already married to a famous lawyer in New York. Bea, I reply: You've forgotten the time difference again. Sorry, she says, but I had a nightmare. I woke up bathed in sweat. I saw you, with a young man. You and he were a couple. You looked in complete despair! Ideal candidates for Brooklyn Bridge. Typical Bea. She thought something had happened to me. Since she's been in America she thinks that people are dying like flies. Her relations, her friends. She must be very lonely. I mean, so very alone.

She studies him.

Neat coat.

DIONYSOS. My mother's. Goatskin.

ISA. Goatskin! This guy's wearing a goatskin! You must've been the one in her dream, I'm sure. She's got sixth sense. Always knew when the phone was going to ring and stuff . . .

A mobile phone rings in her handbag, she starts, answers the phone.

Okay, I'm coming.

She puts the phone away.

My father. Got to go. Do you have any time free?

DIONYSOS. Time is something I have in abundance.

ISA. Shall we swap addresses?

DIONYSOS. I prefer my own company.

ISA. Do you have a coin?

He gives her one, she throws the coin into the trench. Out of it shines a golden light. Both of them lean over the edge.

Building sites are the most beautiful things in this city.

The ground breaks. They fall into the trench.

1 A Winter Evening

A stairwell in need of repair. Ground floor. Entry to the building is marked by the front of the stage. On the left a door leading to a flat with 'DIONYSOS' chalked on it. Opposite is a door leading into the courtyard. Upstage right in front of the fireproof wall is a circular staircase leading to the top floors. In the middle of the wall is a window, behind which can be seen the backs of houses. Underneath the stairs are steps which lead down into the cellar. On the right wall is a row of letter boxes.

ISA *is sitting on the window bench and is holding a handkerchief to her swollen lip. She is smoking and reading a travel brochure at the same time.* KETTLING *is standing on the stairs with his trouser legs up, polishing his shoes. He is wearing a suit, a turban, a neon tie and gold spectacles. On the ground next to him are various presents and carrier bags. Outside it is evening. Snowflakes.*

ISA (*turning over the pages, reads*). Hebron – and what would you do?

KETTLING. Not smoke. Not smoke and not drink. No drugs.

ISA. What would you do differently to Abraham?

KETTLING. Which Abraham?

ISA. The one we all come from.

KETTLING. Man is descended from apes.

ISA (*looks out of the window*). Sixteenth of December. Everything looks normal. White flakes, huge flakes. As big as babies' heads. A few moments ago it was all grey and then suddenly the world is white.

KETTLING. Typical December.

ISA. Right. So far nothing unusual. The first snow – and everything is blooming.

KETTLING. Each day your world comes closer to the end.

ISA. One look at the sky's enough. The stars are dwindling.

KETTLING. Stars don't die. Stars live for ever. Even if they're extinguished, they still survive. As a black hole. Nothing gets lost. Where would it go?

ISA. No mother, no brother, no sisters, my best friend's married . . .

KETTLING. You do have a father. Not a traditional one, admittedly.

ISA. No family!

KETTLING. Isabella, you're divided. Two or three in one, not enough room. That's why nothing is ever enough for you.

He smells her breath.

You've been drinking. Where were you last night?

She doesn't reply.

You're missing a tooth, your handbag . . .

ISA. Nothing. No-one. You've got dirt on your shoes.

KETTLING (*polishing his shoes*). This town is the most perfect example of the modern world: a gold mine. Right in the heart of Europe. As a man of the times, one has to roll up one's trouser legs, stand in the current and prospect.

ISA. Four million people are circling around each other like planets. Waterless planets! Don't like talking, prefer to be alone . . .

KETTLING (*folds up his duster*). Planets don't circle around each other. Moons circle around planets. And planets around stars. Double stars are the ones that change. Their state fluctuates.

He opens the window.

Look at that star there. Yesterday it was shining, today it's dull. Unarmed, one could believe it was fading. But armed with a telescope one can see why.

He pulls a telescope out of his pocket and inspects the heavens.

A second star, invisible to the naked eye, has pushed itself in front of the first star, so the first one appears darker. If a third star was circling around the second one and made a shadow, this would also affect the first star. In short: it is impossible to assess the relationship between multiple stars.

ISA. You and your star-gazing.

KETTLING. Who is he? What kind of black hole is swallowing my little star up.

ISA. No-one. Nothing.

She leafs through a few more pages.

Those three gods that visited Abraham in Sodom – what would you have said to them?

KETTLING. God is dead. There is no God. The world is pure fluke.

ISA. Fluke?

KETTLING. Don't worry. I control the future. I'll buy the

house. You can have the loft. I'll convert it. A paradise for my angel.

ISA. Thank you.

KETTLING. And I'll buy the one next door too. The whole complex. Peanuts!

Dust falls from the wall. He collects it.

Forty years of appalling planning.

He blows the dust out of the window and then closes it.

Everything is under emergency management. The freehold still needs sorting. I'll sort it.

ISA. Four presents, a trip to the Red Sea, a house, a dress, driving lessons . . .

KETTLING. Five. I've taken some tiger tail.

ISA. Tiger tail?

KETTLING. An aphrodisiac. Imported from Asia. Two thousand marks a gram.

He puts his arm around her.

So we can be like a pair of tigers in the jungle, far away from civilisation . . .

ISA. Father.

KETTLING. I know, true love knows no boundaries. Yet a man like myself has some scruples. You're eighteen today. My conscience acquits me at least halfway.

ISA. I'm moving out.

KETTLING. I see.

ISA. Bea left home at 17.

KETTLING. So suddenly.

ISA. I've come of age.

KETTLING. Of course.

He picks up the bags and the dress.

And El Khalil?

ISA. You and your Porsche.

She gives him the brochures.

I don't want to go to Hebron.

KETTLING. Let's eat. With Moosbach. I'll wait for you in the car.

Off, carrying the bags, boxes and dress.

ISA (*looking out of the window*). Paradise! In reality it's a nightmare. A few moments ago it was freezing, now it's minus five. Stormy and depressingly grey. The new snow has turned the courtyard into a slimy desert. This is not a world for me.

She pulls two pistols out of her pocket, puts one in her mouth and the other one at the back of her head.
DIONYSOS *comes up from the cellar, a plaster over one eye, laden down with boxes. He opens the door to his flat without noticing* ISA *and disappears into it.*

ISA (*taking hold of her hair*). His hair, it's just like mine. He looks like me. He really looks like me.

She runs out into the courtyard and off. The stage remains empty.

MANIA, *in her pyjamas, a duvet under her arm, comes down the stairs. She knocks on the flat door.*

MANIA. Hey, Dionysos – the small light that shines in your eyes, well, I'm a moth. Let me in.

DIONYSOS *opens the door and disappears immediately back inside, where we see him packing.* MANIA *leans against the door, and pulls a cigarette out of her pocket.*

Got a light?

DIONYSOS. No.

MANIA. You're leaving? Where you off to?

DIONYSOS. I'm giving up the flat.

MANIA. Going abroad?

DIONYSOS. Perhaps a year on an oilrig. They need people like me.

MANIA. You're a typical representative of the lost generation. Nothing you do has any future in it. Does your mother still give you money?

DIONYSOS. Off and on.

MANIA. That's enough.

DIONYSOS. The house is being sold off. An investor from the west is raping the entire complex. He's going to blow up the blocks at the back. Grass them over. Green over the terraces too – for the tax incentives. The shoe repair man across the road's gone already.

MANIA. Sometimes renovation can be a good thing for the tenants. Okay, you might live on a building site for eight or nine months, after that the future looks bright and beautiful.

DIONYSOS. Exactly, flash cars parked in double rows, restaurants overflowing with childless double income couples in designer clothes. People whose favourite hobbies are shopping and consuming.

MANIA (*goes to the window and looks out*). The block at the back is empty. The block at the back and that one on the side. Used to be a sweet dog there.

DIONYSOS. Always had bronchitis. In September, November and December.

MANIA. Used to be home to forty units. Zielinski, Marder, Stefanek. All pensioners, all swept away. Eight thousand of them, compensated and then imprisoned in tower blocks.

She opens the window, leans out.

Soon the last airway will be blocked. Another office tower. And towering above that – a crane. They stand around the city like King Kongs, nothing but enormous gorillas. They're doing my head in.

She closes the window.

We're staying, Michel and I. My tenancy is twenty years old.

She goes over to the door, leans against the frame.

Can I sleep with you? There's nobody on the second floor, or the fourth or the fifth. No Uwe, no Astrid. Dirk left last week, he was afraid of the rent going up.

DIONYSOS. You do nothing but sleep.

MANIA. Addicted to sleep. Get up at midday. Drink an empty cup of tea, listen to music – without turning it on, write letters without ink – it starts to get difficult with the date. Take a brush, paint – just stripes and you've got a zebra . . . I've had nothing to do for six years, Michel for five. If you don't do anything, you lose all sense of identity.

DIONYSOS. You've got a flat.

MANIA. Occupied occasionally by a woman and a fly. I'm the woman.

DIONYSOS. Where's Michel?

MANIA. Flown away. Won't be back today. Just phoned. He's through to the second interview with Continent. They offer a parcel service. Loads of famous racing drivers. And as I was saying well-done for his partial success at the interview, that little word 'future' popped out – happiness is elsewhere.

DIONYSOS. You had a fight?

MANIA. We're in the most beautiful city in the world and we fight. We're in the largest piazza in the world and we fight. We're in the best bar in the city and we fight, snow's falling, there are bombs on Baghdad, doesn't matter what: we fight. He explodes. I have only to say the word 'future' and he goes straight off like a mixture of nitro-glycerine and potassium cyanide . . .

DIONYSOS (*coming to the door*). Look, Mania, sometimes I'm down too.

MANIA. No-one lives here any more, apart from us . . .

DIONYSOS. And so I stand on my doorstep and gobble down the words of my neighbour like a hungry wolf.

MANIA. Bon appetit!

DIONYSOS. But I prefer to be alone.

MANIA. What's that, above your eye?

DIONYSOS. A cut. I fell into a hole in the ground.

MANIA. On your own?

DIONYSOS. With a woman.

MANIA. And what happened before that?

DIONYSOS. Nothing.

MANIA. Afterwards?

DIONYSOS. Casualty.

MANIA. BSE. I saw my first case yesterday. The number plate on a car B-SE. Only in Berlin. Got a light?

DIONYSOS. No.

He closes the door.

MANIA. Where's the spark? The flickering flame against modern hysteria and life's worries.

She walks to the post boxes, unlocks one. A pile of letters and junk mail falls out. She gathers them up. KETTLING enters, a package under his arm. MANIA greets him vaguely whilst skimming through her post. He goes to the stair-window, opens it, and looks up at the sky. She closes the box. After a while she places herself next to him.

MANIA (*after some time*). Do you have a light? I've got arms and legs like cucumbers, but no light.

KETTLING (*pulls out a lighter*). Venus is about to rise.

MANIA. Venus?

KETTLING. Goddess of love. Do you want a look?

MANIA. Love to. How?

KETTLING (*pulls the telescope out of his pocket*). Be my guest.

MANIA takes the telescope and inspects the sky.

MANIA. I'm in dire need of a ray of sunshine. Situation's desperate. The heaven's the same colour as a drain cover. Perhaps the world begins beyond this heaven, and we are in hell.

KETTLING. Quite possibly.

Takes the telescope.

May I? It's a telescope, not a magnifying glass.

Turns it around so she's looking through the right end.

How did you fall from heaven, shining morning star? That's what Isaiah asked himself.

MANIA. Who?

KETTLING. Venus is a wandering star with different phases. It changes, like the moon. Even the Brahmans didn't know about Venus. Didn't appear until the Babylonians. But then in duplicate. A morning star and evening star. From Ishkatar to Akkad it rose in the west, from Ishkatar to Erech in the east. Two stars, two gods. Unification happened with the Sumerians.

MANIA. Unification?

KETTLING. Two godheads, put together into one Aphrodite-like archetype: Venus. About to rise. And then it leaves us again. In darkest, hopeless night. Which only goes to show that love is a twilight zone that leads into absolute darkness.

MANIA. I can't see either. No evening star, no morning star. No star at all.

KETTLING (*pulls a dress out of the box*). Do you like it?

MANIA. Lovely. Looks expensive.

KETTLING. I've got the dress. But not the woman to go.

MANIA (*takes a cigarette*). Berlin is as cold as Casablanca. But the women are romantic. Do you have a light?

KETTLING. Put it on.

MANIA. What?

KETTLING (*slaps her face*). I don't ask twice. Put it on.

Takes the duvet off her and holds it up.

You can go behind this paravent. Do it behind this paravent.

MANIA. Rape?

He does not reply.

And in order to say that you needed the Sumerians, Brahmans . . .

KETTLING. Put it on. And nothing underneath.

She puts the dress on. He holds the duvet up, looking out of the window.

Lovestar! A cheerless planet, according to today's experts. Permanent heat, night and day. Permanent cloud cover. The heavens never open up, no window to the universe, no light from space. A climactic catastrophe every day: greenhouse effect.

Lowers the cover.

You're beautiful, Isa.

MANIA. I'm not Isa.

KETTLING (*slaps her face*). Did I ask you?

He spreads the duvet over the stairs, pulls out his shoe cleaning cloth.

Sorry. But people like you usually have lungs like Pavarotti, despite your delicate appearance.

He gags her with the shoe cleaning cloth, stands expectantly.

Fight me off.

She remains motionless.

Lie down.

She lies down on the steps.

Open your legs.

She does so. He lies on top of her.

Fight me off.

She remains motionless.

Go on, fight me off.

She doesn't move.

Who told you to lie still?

She doesn't move. He sits down on the steps.

Who do you think I am? Some dickhead with a Porsche?

MANIA (*pulling the gag out of her mouth*). Porsche?

KETTLING. Moosbach says: you feel guilty at the death of your wife, because YOUR mother threw herself off a bridge. You feel guilty about the educational performance of your daughter, because YOU left school at 16. You feel guilty about your private wealth, the 90 million marks . . .

MANIA. Ninety million?

KETTLING. All of which means that I'm just like my father. Depressing.

Takes the shoe cleaning cloth, folds it up.

You didn't know grandfather. Alois Vollbrecht – 'Reverential piano tuning'. He started small. At the end of his life he had an emporium: furniture, investment and so on. I was the only heir. Of course I had to destroy his illusions, as a protest. I played at being a radical student. A Trotzkyist funded by the state and my grandmother. Fifteen years later I went back into the business. Because of my passion for Porsches. For nought to sixty in six, I betrayed the revolution permanently. Yes, I'm guilty. Of prosperity, of neglect.

He puts the cloth back into his pocket.

It's all in the genes.

MANIA. Ninety million. Genetically.

KETTLING. Science calls it: reproduction.

MANIA. A Porsche, reproduced. What's your number plate?

KETTLING. An Osnabrück number. Who are you?

MANIA. Mania. I live here.

KETTLING. Take the dress off.

She takes it off, she's got pyjamas on underneath.

What was I talking about?

MANIA. Unification.

KETTLING. Sorry. I've been drinking. No, I want to be honest: I took a consciousness-changing drug: Tiger tail. Anything else happen?

MANIA. Nope. Nothing.

KETTLING. No hope from Asia then. Are you from the west or east?

MANIA. East.

KETTLING. Pity. What should come from the heart comes out of the mouth.

He sets off, then stops.

Unification will come from the children of unification. That's what I believe.

Exits, carrying box and dress. MANIA *pulls a cigarette out of her pyjamas.* MICHEL *enters, wearing a striped t-shirt, leather jacket, trainers, rucksack.*

MANIA. Back already.

MICHEL. Got to go again.

MANIA. Nothing changes. The usual thing. How did it go at Continent?

MICHEL. The biggest plans get lost in time.

He gives her a small packet.

MANIA. Yogi tea.

MICHEL. Read the label.

MANIA (*reading*). Compassion – the key to happiness.

MICHEL. Small packet. Great wisdom. Great, ancient wisdom. Mania, I . . .

MANIA. Michel, I'm over thirty. Time to take stock. Seven years together. What does the future hold?

MICHEL. Future?

He goes up the steps and sits on the window bench.

Look, Mania, you stand at the station waiting for a train you know you've already missed; you're on the platform and you can actually see the rearlights of the train, you know you'll never catch it, and so you start thinking. The thoughts dance, like a swarm of midges and you set about swatting them. What happens then – they attack.

He looks out of the window.

Have you noticed there are no rats here? In other old blocks the rats creep into the flats through the toilets. Not here. In other courtyards they jump out from gaping sewage covers and bite the inhabitants on the leg. But not here. People say there's a rat for every inhabitant in Berlin because it's just one big building site. The noise is sawing up their souls. In panic they're reproducing manically. Sewage rats react to a disturbed life by multiplying blindly: rattus norwegicus. So why don't we have any rats? Because they've all been eaten by cats. Good thing too, that's what you're thinking. But what has happened to the fleas?

MANIA. What fleas?

MICHEL. The fleas in the cats' fur. Plague-carrying fleas.

MANIA. Plague-carrying fleas, in cats?

MICHEL. The rider of the apocalypse is at the front of the grid: black death is galloping onwards, and recently it has arrived at our latitude. Lot's carriers are rats, cats, people.

MANIA. What does that mean for the future?

MICHEL. Typhus, plague and cholera are knocking at Central Europe's door and all you can think of is the future?

MANIA. My future, Michel. Not Central Europe's.

MICHEL. Malaria.

MANIA. Malaria?

MICHEL. Perhaps you've got malaria. You put your feelings above reason, Mania, like you've got a high fever. The future! You've got future madness!

He looks out of the window.

It's the weather's fault. The weather, the warmth. One degree warmer and they'll be climbing out of the stinking swamps of the trenches. One degree warmer and the swarms of Anopheles will be carrying out the Last Judgement.

MANIA. Why do you think it's the weather, Michel?

MICHEL. Gaming. I made a bet.

MANIA. I knew it!

MICHEL. Yes, I made a bet! On everything, even the weather. Finally, despite every forecast, I put money on the sun shining.

Looks out of the window.

Rain. For weeks now. The drains are kaput. It's dripping through a sieve and spraying in all directions. Just like my life. No peace, no river, no sleep. No rain. Rain is nothing but piss in disguise.

He smashes in a window pane with his fist.

MANIA. You gambled.

MICHEL. Gambled and lost.

MANIA. In order to tell me that you had to bring in the end of the world?

MICHEL. No small reason.

MANIA. The appointment with Continent?

MICHEL. Missed it.

MANIA. Through to the second phase?

MICHEL. As the first one started, I was at rock bottom.

MANIA. You were going to catch up?

MICHEL. Save your interest. I don't deserve it. Higher you climb, further you fall. Mania, you have to leave me.

MANIA. Leave? That's not in my power. We have to start the future now, Michel. This very moment, a new life.

He's silent.

A poetic moment.

MICHEL. No future, Mania. It's over. Forget me. Be happy. You're a beautiful woman.

MANIA. What are you going to do?

MICHEL. No fixed address, no fixed girlfriend, no address in space . . .

MANIA. Tramp . . .

MICHEL. My perspective: life on the street. Don't worry. You'll never see me sitting at the exit to some tube.

MANIA. Where will you go?

MICHEL. Away from Berlin, away from building works. I'll be homeless elsewhere.

MANIA. Your things?

MICHEL. I'll pick them up later. Don't need them. If I take a bus to the station, I'll just catch the night train. A pity the Volvo's gone.

MANIA. Yup, a pity.

MICHEL. I could have waited till morning if we still had the Volvo.

MANIA. What does this mean for the future?

MICHEL. Nothing. You're a good person.

Exits.

A bright light comes in through the window.

MANIA. Venus – amazing, what a light.

Reads the package again.

Compassion! I showed compassion, my love, for seven years. I bore the cost of our unit.

She throws the packet away. Pulls a piece of paper out of her pocket.

Week of action. Your chance to . . . uh, they shouldn't keep sending me these pieces of paper. I always take the printed word so seriously.

Throws the piece of paper away, takes a cigarette, realises she doesn't have a light.

Help!

2 A Winter's Morning

The same stairwell. Soft morning light.

MICHEL *is sticking a plastic bag over the smashed pane of glass.* MANIA, *in her pyjamas, comes out of* DIONYSOS' *flat, closes the door quietly behind her – then notices* MICHEL.

MICHEL. He's still asleep?

MANIA. He . . .

MICHEL (*interrupting her*). . . . is your cousin.

MANIA. I . . .

MICHEL. . . . don't have a thing going with him. You always say that.

MANIA. It's . . .

MICHEL. not what I think. I know –

He touches his forehead.

Horns. Insects have feelers, the men from Mars have antennae. So much is not what one thinks. For example, the train timetable. It was wrong. The train only went as far as Braunschweig. So I slept the night on a station bench in Braunschweig. Hibernated in a waiting room. Came back to Berlin with the first train. Flat was empty. In the cafés night was being shooed out. Only a very short night between yesterday and this morning. Radical changes usually hit fast.

MANIA. We . . .

MICHEL. . . . were like children. I know. You were lonely, he was alone. So, a case of eastalgia.

MANIA. For God's sake, Michel!

MICHEL. Such happy memories, I'm right, aren't I? Where do you both come from? Karl-Marx-Town? Lenindorf?

MANIA (*crossing her arms*). We . . .

MICHEL. . . . West Germans are nuts. I know, mad cow's disease. That's what you think. You, on the other hand, know what it is to have a heart: solidarity. Support not sex. A sense of comradeship, great comradeship. Why be jealous? Life is too short.

MANIA. You . . .

MICHEL. . . . East Germans are not fixed on personal possessions. I know.

MANIA (*crossing her arms*). So . . .

MICHEL. . . . You weren't quite sure. Better that way. Better to say nothing.

MANIA. Look . . .

MICHEL (*interrupting her*). You're not going to allow me to keep you quiet, I know.

She remains silent.

Mania, if I'm not letting you get a word in edgeways, it's because I'm speechless. Really speechless.

Looks out of the window.

The events of last night can't be changed. What does it prove? It proves that he likes you. I like you too. And the rest? If there was a reckoning, one thing is sure, I've lost. Perhaps if I gave myself an advance. I know happy couples are in the minority. As are perfect couples and normal relationships. But to forget. Going up and down these stairs every day, every step reminding me: here went the woman that I loved. No, don't probe. I know you haven't changed. The circumstances have, but not you. The circumstances are no longer what they were last night.

MANIA (*to herself*). Push this love to one side. Stamp on the cockroach. Put a stake through the vampire. This relationship is like a zombie. It's not alive and it's not dead either. Michel, I'm leaving you – that's what I should say to him. And then I'll write to my mother: Coming home. Need some hugs. Love Mania.

To MICHEL.

Michel, I'm leaving you.

MICHEL. Perhaps you're sleep-talking? Open-eyed, you're sitting, walking, standing, talking. Let us speak in the language of sharks.

He sticks some sellotape over her mouth, puts his hands around her throat and pushes her slowly to the floor.

A ship is sinking. The old shark says to the young ones: Okay boys, you know the routine – women and children first. Have you ever seen my fangs?

He continues to throttle her, then drops her. Walks to the window and looks out. She lies on the floor, motionless.

No chainsaw, no meat cleaver in my hand. A truly suburban hell.

MANIA (*removing the sticky tape from her mouth*). Why do you come back? Again and again?

MICHEL. I like my flat.

MANIA. It's my flat. I signed the contract.

MICHEL. My bed. I need my bed.

MANIA. You're so middle class.

She stands up.

MICHEL. It's my childhood, you know. Small town in western Germany close to the Dutch border. Time at my grandmother's. A few years locked in there. Then school, followed by further years of imprisonment. I'm conditioned to live in a cell.

MANIA. The electricity bill came yesterday. We owe them an extra 2000 marks.

MICHEL. We love each other. We hurt each other.

MANIA. Day before yesterday it was the gas bill. The deposit for the coming year.

MICHEL. Electricity, gas, telephone. You ask a lot from a modern nineties man, Mania, too much.

MANIA. Tell me that you love me.

MICHEL. My heart's holding a consultation. My lips . . .

He touches his lips.

. . . are sealed. Three short words. My heart says, yes. My lips? Apathetic.

MANIA. Always the same. Nothing ever changes.

MICHEL. There were Amazons, Mania, who tied the unfaithful in a piece of cloth and threw them into the river. Stopped the men from crying.

MANIA. Our love is more complicated.

MICHEL. Far too complicated.

MANIA. You and your blind jealousy. I'm going to cut the pair of you loose, like snipping a dead leaf from a tree.

She puts her hand out.

The key. To the cellar. My suitcases are in the cellar.

MICHEL (*holds onto her hand*). Look Mania, if everything was a bit clearer, a bit more comprehensible. I'd be a different man, I'd tie every morning afresh onto yesterday. I don't have a job.

MANIA. My days are grey too. The world's missing.

MICHEL. In the middle of the night I wake up, toss and turn. When the others get out of bed, I finally go to sleep. Only to find myself standing in the kitchen much later on with nothing to do, and I have to ask myself: what day is it today?

MANIA. A glance at the calendar might help, Michel.

MICHEL. I can't sleep any more.

MANIA. And I can't do anything but sleep.

MICHEL. I went to university. Studied the arts, got my degree, did a doctorate and that was that. So made my hobby into my profession. Welding, design. "Merchandise by Michel". Mornings, I sit on my furniture in a room with two windows, both of them with a view of another wall.

MANIA. You should keep taking photos. You're multi-talented.

MICHEL. Ruined houses. Broken, just like our lives. Who wants to look at that?

MANIA. You feel so sorry for yourself. So sorry.

MICHEL. Mania, there are ways of dying that don't wait for the body to turn into a corpse. I don't need to kill myself. I'm dead already.

MANIA. The key to the cellar.

He takes two keys off his ring. MANIA *goes into the cellar.* MICHEL *opens the window which looks onto the courtyard and looks out. Outside, birds are singing.*

MICHEL. Starlings in December. Too late.

He leans out of the window.

In Spring I'm going to grass over the courtyard. Plant a tree. Should do that, once in a lifetime. And water carefully. In this terrible heat. Young trees don't survive that sort of heat. The following year they're leafless. And what's my New Year's wish? No gaps, no freewheeling. I want to work.

He lies down on the bench in front of the window.

Work is a curse. No-one works in paradise.

He falls asleep.

MANIA *returns from the cellar with two suitcases.*

MANIA. Get up. Or you'll get stuck there.

MICHEL. Life's not being kind to me today.

MANIA. I want another kind of life.

MICHEL. Mania, I had a dream. The unemployed were lying on a sand dune like sea lions.

MANIA. I want to change it, my life.

MICHEL. And what about the future, Mania?

Suddenly from outside: a pneumatic drill.

MANIA. This used to be a dozy country.

MICHEL. Somebody was telling me recently that he always hears pneumatic drills. Wherever he goes, whenever he stops, he hears a pneumatic drill. He thinks it's building works. But during the night?

He closes the window.

Mania, we're staying.

MANIA. We . . . ?

Exits up the stairs. MANIA *sits on a suitcase and pulls a cigarette out of her dressing gown pocket.* ISA *enters in an elegant black fur coat with a suitcase in her hand. She doesn't notice* MANIA, *instead pulls an envelope out of her pocket then studies the names on the letter boxes.*

ISA. Meier, Müller, Schmidt.

MANIA. Looking for someone?

ISA (*startled*). Me? Looking? No.

MANIA. It's hard for me, his unhappiness. A confused man.

ISA. Who?

MANIA. My partner.

ISA. Do you live here?

MANIA. Upstairs. Happiness is his enemy.

ISA. Happiness?

MANIA. The state of the world plays its part too.

ISA. Do you live together?

MANIA. Not any more. I'm going back to the Spreewald. That's where I come from: I was a gymnast. A red star in my hairband, I wanted to backflip around the world. Never got that far. Private tuition costs thirty thousand.

ISA (*pulls a bundle of banknotes out of her bag. Throws them in the air*). Here's ten. Ten thousand marks.

MANIA (*unimpressed*). Got a light?

ISA. I don't smoke. Or do I? I've forgotten.

She reads the name on the flat door.

Dionysos – do you think he's in love with me?

MANIA. He won't love another woman as long as his mother's alive.

ISA. His mother?

MANIA. A writer. His affairs are merely phases.

ISA. Gay?

MANIA. Oedipus could certainly shine a light on the matter.

ISA. Detective Isa on the case!

She turns her collar up.

I'll transport myself into the person I'm observing. Looks, walk, gestures. The whole shebang. So: male body language. His heels go click clack. Click clack! And you can forget about smiling. He looks out from the middle of his skull. His eyelids droop. Well, sort of. Always spreads his legs when he sits. Even on the tube, against your seat . . . do I look like him?

MANIA. Apart from the cut.

ISA. We fell into a trench. Nothing happened before that, afterwards there was just the doctor. Odd.

MANIA. Is there anything that isn't odd? How old are you?

ISA. Twenty-five. Eighteen.

MANIA. Eighteen. And throwing your money around like that.

ISA. Have you ever been in love?

MANIA. I thought I was.

ISA. Any lesbian experiences?

MANIA. Women have tried it on. But seriously? No,

ISA. Where's your partner?

MANIA. Upstairs. Resting.

ISA (*looking at the door*). Dionysos – Greek?

MANIA. Not sure.

ISA. Until today I lived with Daddy. A hundred and seventy square metres in a loft. There was a lift thrown in, and an au pair for the Afghans. Daddy used to be a Trotzkyist. Has a good heart, though. Protects me, shields me. The world is so rough. He's okay. Apart from one thing: he always falls asleep in front of me. Jabbers away at me, on anything from fucking to philosophers, then dozes off and I'm left with my eyes wide open. Leaves me alone with the night, says goodbye by falling asleep . . .

MANIA. In whose bed does your father lie, when he talks to you about his problems?

ISA. In ours.

MANIA. Do you also sleep in this communal bed?

ISA. I moved out this morning.

MANIA. Does he abuse you?

ISA. You mean, do I sleep with him? Sadly no, nor with anyone else. Dionysos, he looks really sweet to me. Do you think I'm in love with him?

MANIA. Only your heart can tell you that. What does your father look like?

ISA. Good-looking. Like an Arab. A prince from the United Arab Emirates. And he does everything for me. I wanted a camel for Christmas. He gave me a herd. They're grazing somewhere even now. In some sort of a desert. I'll see them next summer.

MANIA. And what did you give him?

ISA. A neon tie. He runs around in it as proudly as Aquamarina in her collar.

MANIA. Aquamarina?

ISA. An Afghan hound. Not from Afghanistan.

MANIA. Dior on the outside, a desert inside.

She stands up and picks up her suitcase.

My father, Otto Bigallke, was a communist. First a communist, then a socialist and now a capitalist. At present he is a temp at the city waste disposal unit in Finsterluckenau. He's a good man. A very good man. Because all through his life he's avoided meat. Particularly beef, British beef. We couldn't get hold of it. The whole of the Eastern block is BSE free.

She gets up to leave.

ISA. Don't forget the money. Ten thousand, for the journey. A present!

MANIA. What do you want? A Mercedes? Another credit card? Money might be lying on the street, we know that. But my partner and I, we're not the sort of people who bend down to pick it up.

She tries to leave.

ISA. I thought you'd split up.

MANIA. You know what. We live in houses ringed with entrances, surrounded by exits. It can happen that one door jams. But another one soon springs open.

ISA. Get to the point.

MANIA. The point? The point is that there are more important things than wealth, travel and money. Love – purifies everything. Who said that? St Paul?

ISA. No idea. The pope!

She laughs out loud, hitting her arms.

Don't get hysterical now.

MANIA. You're hysterical! You and your money!

MANIA *leaves, going up the stairs.* ISA *studies the letter boxes. Finally she knocks on the flat door.*

ISA. Dionysos?

She knocks.

It's me, Isa.

She knocks.

We fell into a trench together.

She listens, smiles, leans against the door.

What sort of a man is he, I wonder. Bit of a hippy? Sells stuff at flea markets? Or maybe he didn't finish his degree and now lives with his parents? Perhaps he was a taxi-driver, lost his licence. Been in a bad mood since. Doesn't like talking. Prefers to be alone. Is he moody? Thunder, lightening, depression. Sorry, I mean melancholic . . .

She listens, knocks. No reaction. She leans against the door.

Does he get money from his granny? Is he unhinged, rotting in there like a tipped-up biotope?

She walks up and down.

I just met Miss Bigallke. So now I know everything about you.

Behind the door a cup falls. She smiles.

You want to run and run and run through the dark streets without stopping. You walk, without talking, to anyone. And the more you see, the more you have to run because your spirit won't rest. Just like me. We're about the same age. Your father left your family when you were still small. After the death of your mother you moved here.

DIONYSOS (*opening the door*). Mother's alive. What do you want?

ISA. I'm interested in your country. Especially the Greek hospitality.

DIONYSOS *sweeps up the broken pieces.*

You are Greek, aren't you?

DIONYSOS. Half.

ISA. Brothers or sisters?

DIONYSOS. Only Greeks, I don't know them.

ISA. What does your father do?

DIONYSOS. Unknown.

ISA. Yet fathers are so important. Irreplaceable. Like mothers, in fact. Sometimes I feel like an unmanned ship roaming the ocean alone. Dionysos – unusual name for around here. What occurs to you when I say the word, mother?

DIONYSOS. I prefer to spend my mornings alone.

He tries to close the door, she puts her foot in.

ISA. Someone laughs, someone else cries. One person is sad, the other merry. One person is worried, someone else comforts them. After a bit of television, a quick bath, good night and off to bed?

DIONYSOS. What do you want? Asking questions which can't be answered?

ISA (*gives him the letter*). For you. There was no name on the box. I've set down my feelings in black and white.

He opens it and reads.

Didn't know how to start, so went for the clichés.

DIONYSOS. You write that we're friends?

ISA. I'd prefer to read it out loud myself.

She takes the letter from him.

So, to keep it brief, we're related. Soul siblings. You're like me. We're like each other. And like likes to dock onto like. Germany to Germany. Mercedes to Benz. Our souls streamed out last night and bound us together. You want proof? The William Tell test.

She pulls out a pistol.

I read about it in a magazine.

She hands him the pistol.

An old FN-Browning. Very rare. Father always says I should collect something.

She walks away from him and turns around, puts an apple on her head and closes her eyes.

Shoot.

DIONYSOS. Isabella.

ISA. Isa. Bella sounds so stupid.

DIONYSOS. Whatever you're called. Do it yourself.

ISA. Shoot!

DIONYSOS. I'm an anti-fascist. I was never in the army.

ISA. Never in the army? What about national service?

DIONYSOS. We could choose. Borstal or barracks. So I chose. I turned down any service that had to do with weapons.

ISA. It's quite simple.

She pulls a second pistol out of her coat pocket.

Stretch out your right arm, your left hand supports the wrist. Close one eye and aim with the other and . . .

She fires a shot into the doorframe. DIONYSOS *drops to the floor. As he does so his own gun goes off.* ISA *drops to the floor. After a pause.*

That was some shot. People will talk about that.

She stands up and picks up the apple with the hole in it.

You've passed the Tell-test. A had blind faith, B had an unerring heart. That proves you love me. Even if your voice is silent, your soul was speaking to me, quite clearly.

DIONYSOS (*still on the floor*). What do you want?

ISA (*picking up her suitcase*). Want? Need. I'll reveal all once I've moved in.

DIONYSOS. Moved in? Mother will have a fit.

ISA. Mother?

She helps him up, takes the pistol off him.

There are much higher powers at work here. The fall into that trench, what was that, nothing?

DIONYSOS. Hardly extraordinary. Berlin is one big building site.

ISA. Fluke perhaps?

DIONYSOS. To believe in divine providence at this point would be premature, I feel. Besides, I prefer my own company.

He disappears into the flat. ISA *follows him with her bags. She closes the door. The stage is empty.*

MANIA *comes down the steps, makes sure she's alone, then collects up the money.*

Suddenly the stage shakes, the windows spring open. Outside there is the sound of building works. MANIA *looks out.*

MANIA. They're coming. King Kongs.

She pulls a cigarette out of her pyjamas.

If only I had a light . . .

The block of flats at the back explodes.

3 Christmas Eve

The same stairwell, only now it's more like a building site. The plaster has been knocked off the walls, there are planks on the floor, a wheelbarrow, sacks of cement. Scaffolding everywhere. Outside through the window, scaffolding and cranes are visible. Everything has Christmas trees on it.

In the middle of the floor is a Christmas tree. MICHEL *is sitting on the window bench with a letter in his hand, a crate of beers next to him. On the steps, between the packages and carrier bags,* MANIA *is kneeling with a new television on her knee. She is trying to get a signal from the satellite dish she's holding over her head.*

MICHEL. Christmas Eve, shortly before four, quickly bought some decorations, a couple of candles and the tree, the bare essentials for three quiet days, come home and find a notice to terminate the tenancy is in the letter box.

He looks out of the window.

There's only one solution, treat life as a joke. The modern experience.

MANIA (*looking for a signal*). The programme's about to start. This is in my blood.

MICHEL. Surrounded by scaffolding, totally enclosed. We're being armed for life. What does it mean, I ask myself, when there are builders swarming outside the windows like gorillas. A life in a cage.

Opens a bottle.

Where's the cousin? Not seen him for days. He used to sit down every evening between us and fill his face, your adoptive son.

MANIA. Leave him alone. He's ill. Trying to get over an affair. Her name's Isa, not from around here. Didn't know anyone in this town.

MICHEL. So how did he meet her?

MANIA. They fell into a trench together. Thirty-six hours later she moved in. Two or three days after that she disappeared, never to be seen again. Didn't leave an address, didn't say good-bye. It's affected his voice. Bad bronchitis, scratchy throat and then suddenly, no voice at all.

She gets a picture.

Cracow.

MICHEL. We have debts and you want to travel the world.

Looks out of the window: MANIA *watches television: travel programme.*

MANIA (*watching television*). Lisbon. Before the earthquake.

MICHEL. Lisbon? We'll fly, Mania, on a one-way ticket.

MANIA. We'll fight the notice to quit. We have a secure tenancy. Indefinite, not terminable.

MICHEL. You're the secure tenant. I'm not in the contract.

MANIA (*watching television*). Mount Etna's active. What's the reason?

MICHEL. Non-payment of rent.

She doesn't hear him, changes the programme. From the television we hear a comedy. MICHEL, *beer bottle in his hand, stands behind her and watches television.*

MANIA (*watches television.* MICHEL *turns the television off. Silence*). Non-payment of rent. We paid. Punctually, on the first.

MICHEL. Mania, child, we're out on the street.

MANIA. The direct debits from our account?

MICHEL. Didn't arrive. We don't have an account.

MANIA. And the money in our account?

MICHEL. The bank took it. The bank closed our account.

MANIA. My contract?

MICHEL (*opens up his wallet*). My possessions. One passport, one photo, one driving licence. I've got a sleeping bag upstairs. Good for up to minus twenty. There's room for two – if you want.

MANIA. How long has the rent not been paid?

MICHEL. Ten, twelve months.

MANIA (*tonelessly*). Ten, twelve months.

MICHEL (*studying a photo*). Me, as a child. Pretty boy. Slightly dreamy. Favourite subject? Art, of course. Same nose, same colour eyes.

Looks at the photo in his passport.

Me, now. How quickly it all goes. Two, three scars, unfulfilled wishes. One or two hits below the belt on my CV. Irreparable damage.

MANIA. What about the ten thousand I found?

MICHEL. Lost Mania. Against some arsehole. One of those regular types that never risk anything, never bet, but always win. Small, ugly and meaningless: smug all round. With a burning wish to win. He went through everything. With a coldness that made my heart shrink. I lost my nerve. Sometimes I ask myself, what is stronger, myself or the world? The world, I think.

He looks at his passport.

Michel Maerz, young, intelligent, flexible. Sadly incompatible with the rules governing world markets.

He rips up his passport.

MANIA. Non-payment of rent. Means we'll be chucked out.

MICHEL. That's what they say. Read it yourself.

MANIA (*taking the letter off him*). Where will we go?

MICHEL. When life starts to put serious questions to you that you can't answer, then it doesn't matter where. You're missing the programme.

He turns the television on. From it we hear birdcalls.

There, mud-flats. Our future, Mania, wander into the water like lemmings. Marx saw it all coming. Only capital is free. People are tied to capital. Bio masses. Blood for computers. Globalisation. Capital is sweeping over the country, scattering life, Mania. We're agreed on that, you, me and Marx? Whom you've probably never read. Otherwise it wouldn't have happened.

MANIA. Leave him out of it.

MICHEL (*goes to the window and looks out*). Marx was a melancholic. The idea of class struggle sprung from a manic phase. He had visions: paradise on earth! Marx also understood irony. He was quite right. And because capitalism infiltrates every reality, we as real people in reality are inevitably wrong. Not of this world. The world is all right. Only we are wrong. The wrong in the right.

Drinks.

MANIA. Leave Marx alone.

MICHEL. A prophet! Prophet and philosopher. Same category as Kierkegaard. Darkness, my dear, darkness. The lights at the end of the tunnel are the spotlights of the Intercity 125's. That's what Marx must have meant. Doubters of all countries join together!

MANIA. You drink too much.

Turns the television off. Sits for a few moments in silence.

Magic moments. This staircase makes me sad.

MICHEL. You're reminded. Of your childhood.

MANIA. Sliding down the banisters. Pausing on the way up, to catch your breath. Playing in the hallway when it rained outside.

MICHEL. It's not raining. There's no snow. Too cold.

MANIA. The Bigallkes lived in this block for generations. Made steady progress, from the courtyard at the back, ground floor, to the house at the front, facing south, the sun.

MICHEL. History flows backwards. Backwards towards the water, whence we came.

MANIA (*picking up the television and the key*). Absolutely no joy. One thing is guaranteed, life is pointless.

MANIA *picks up the satellite dish and TV and goes off up the stairs.*

MICHEL (*shouting after her*). Marx came from the West!! From Trier!

To himself.

An old saying occurs to me. A word from Solomon: the only thing that life has to offer is a halfway decent death. Said it to Croesos, I think.

Hangs himself upside down from the scaffolding.
KETTLING *enters. He's wearing the turban and has a goldfish bowl under his arm. From his coat pocket twinkle two champagne goblets.*

KETTLING *(to the goldfish)*. I love you, I love love.

Notices MICHEL.

What are you doing?

MICHEL. This position expresses my anger at the absurdity of existence.

KETTLING *(looking at the beer crate)*. You're drunk.

MICHEL. Soon be smashed, yup. Brain's about to explode.

KETTLING *(to the goldfish in the bowl)*. Don't drink so much.

MICHEL *(folding his hands)*. My final prayer. To which god should I pray? The Christian one? Christ the Redeemer? Buddha?

KETTLING *(looking at his watch)*. I'd make a quick decision if I were you.

MICHEL. To RA, from whose tears man was made?

KETTLING. That takes a while.

MICHEL. Afraid, until death.

KETTLING. You don't get to be centre stage for that long. I need it for the finale.

MICHEL. Mine is also important.

KETTLING. I was with Moosbach.

MICHEL. I read Marx. What should I pray for?

KETTLING. The Mother of Compassion was visiting Moosbach. You want to die? Up to you. Can I ask why?

MICHEL. Been chucked out. For not paying the rent. The bank closed my account. The contract was in my girlfriend's name, Mania Bigallke.

KETTLING. You used to live here?

MICHEL. When I was alive. Maerz. Michel Maerz. Be on my epitaph. I deserved it.

KETTLING. You exaggerate.

MICHEL. Who do you think you are? To say that to someone so close to the end?

KETTLING (*looking at his watch*). Kettling, I . . .

MICHEL (*interrupting*). Dr Kettling?

KETTLING. Bachelor of Science, Holy Stephen . . .

MICHEL (*smiles*). I lie in the arms of Morpheus whilst the Grim Reaper reaches out from the underworld in the guise of the new landlord.

KETTLING. My God! When you're sitting at your desk you don't see the consequences of a signature.

MICHEL. Don't stop. Carry on. I have a weakness for comedy.

KETTLING. What can I do to make you disappear?

MICHEL. What's so pressing?

KETTLING. My happiness. She'll be here any minute. To give a daughter away to a man, have you ever tried that?

MICHEL. A contract. You can write me a contract for the rent. In my name, secure tenancy.

KETTLING *pulls out a pad and pen.*

Two Deutsch Marks per square metre, the old rate of the East.

KETTLING. Perfectly reasonable price.

MICHEL. Not everything was bad. And it has to be renovated, with bath, loo, central heating.

KETTLING (*rips the paper from the pad*). Your contract.

MICHEL *reads the piece of paper and gets down from the scaffolding.*

MICHEL. Thank you, Mohammed.

Picks up the crate and tree. Pauses in front of the window and looks at the Christmas trees outside.

So lovely to see a Christmas tree. The lights so friendly. Gracious and peaceful. Reminds me of my childhood. The dying afternoon of a dying winter day. Me, incarcerated in my playroom and the curtains hanging like nets for a dying sun.

KETTLING (*looking at his watch*). Couldn't you speed up your departure?

MICHEL. Why? Who knows if we'll meet again.

KETTLING (*to himself*). Patience, Kettling. Compassion. Patience.

MICHEL. One more thing. To continue so to speak, with my thoughts. What are we?

KETTLING. Please.

MICHEL. Who are we? Characters in someone else's story? Cartoon figures? At the very most we're just a crucial point in the plot? We are the lowly ones, low value cards to be thrown down from the hand of an unknown god who only plays with trumps.

MICHEL *goes off up the stairs.* KETTLING *puts the goldfish bowl down on the window bench. To the goldfish.*

KETTLING. I love you, love love . . .

ISA *comes in with shopping bags.*

KETTLING. Got everything?

ISA (*looks uncertainly towards the flat door*). Everything.

KETTLING (*checking the bags*). Asparagus, strawberries, champagne.

Opens the bottle.

You're nervous? We've got time. Show your teeth.

She smiles.

Six thousand marks.

The cork flies out.

To Christmas!

ISA. Here, on a building site?

KETTLING (*pulls the goblets out of his pocket and pours the wine*). What do you wish for? Be honest now. Don't say – a family. I can't offer you that sort of happiness. I'm not a conventional father.

He hands her a glass.

Merry Christmas.

They clink glasses. He kisses her. She prolongs the kiss.

That went far. Too far for our relationship.

ISA. Can I take it back?

KETTLING (*loosening his tie*). You're an adult now.

ISA (*kisses him, empties her glass. Firmly*). Merry Christmas. Let's go.

She picks up the bags. KETTLING *stands still, his hands in his trouser pockets.*

KETTLING (*stays where he is*). I can feel it, you want a man. A proper young man around your age.

He glances at the flat door.

That one there, perhaps?

ISA. Where did you get that idea from?

KETTLING. Dionysos – you whispered his name in your sleep. When I opened your eyelids to see what you were dreaming about, there was no white at all. Just blue. The blue of longing. My heart broke. So I went to Moosbach. And there I met the Mother of Compassion – the only thing left is to do what has to be done. Help something along which is not managing very well on its own.

He knocks at the door. DIONYSOS *opens the door in his fur coat, a black scarf around his neck, a guitar in his hand, stands there coughing and signalling that he cannot speak.*

What a sight! A Goth!

ISA. He's not a Goth!

KETTLING. Existentialist, perhaps?

ISA. He always wears his mother's fur coat when it goes below freezing. He's not even aware of it.

KETTLING. Wild hair. Did he fall into a threshing machine?

ISA. It's part of the scene.

KETTLING. Dionysos – that's not a name you usually hear in this town. What do you like about him?

ISA. His voice.

KETTLING. I see. And does he have a profession, your Greek waiter?

ISA. He's not a foreigner. He's from the East.

KETTLING. From the East.

He starts scratching.

And did anything occur between you?

ISA. No, nothing, absolutely nothing.

KETTLING. I can see there are difficulties getting this thing off the ground.

Walks up the steps, sits down on the bench in front of the window and watches the goldfish, scratching himself all the while.

In Moosbach we meditated on life. Together with the Mother of Compassion we considered what we were doing wrong. We love without prior instruction, we start at the wrong end. At the top with the best. Dare to do the most dangerous thing. Start with the beloved. Of course it's a non-starter. You can't drive a Porsche without a driving licence, can you? Love has to start small.

He pulls a moonstone out of his pocket.

Take a stone. Concentrate on it and – love it. You'll see, love will grow. A bit later you can move onto a goldfish. From the microcosm to the macrocosm, according to Moosbach and the Mother. Object of the exercise: love itself, a feeling without an objective.

Scratching himself all over.

From the East, you say?

Scratches himself, looking at the fish.

He's got red in him. Not a good idea to suppress my phobia in Moosbach.

Opens the window and throws the bowl out.

Pigment allergy, that's what the scientists say. Biochemical memory of the good old times. Careful now Kettling, control yourself. Quietly now. Have patience, compassion. Offer a helping hand.

Closes the window. Goes over to ISA, *holds his hands out.*

Flat keys, car keys, credit cards, the lot, please. And the one with the telephone chip. The chip for the city toilets. Pistols, both of them. Mobile phone, handbag, shoes, tights . . .

ISA *gives him everything. He gets out his shoe cleaning cloth.*

And wipe that unbelievably expensive face cream off.

ISA. Not with the cloth you use for cleaning your shoes.

KETTLING (*pauses, smiles*). A present.

He picks up the bags and boxes.

You're quite pretty. A bit dishevelled with your shirt hanging out of your trousers. I was like that, at your age. If I was distraught, that's what I looked like. Like you. There's no need. You don't have to worry about the fact it's Christmas Eve. Or should you?

Smiling, he picks something up from the floor.

A stone. One must start small.

To the stone.

And by the end you can love everything. Even a Greek waiter.

Exits with bags and packages.

ISA. The only thing he hasn't done is send in a killer.

Rubs her freezing arms.

Now I could really do with Bea.

DIONYSOS *gives her his coat. Whispers/coughs something.*

Sleep with you? Thanks a lot.

DIONYSOS *whispers/coughs.*

Shy? Have you got a screw loose? You're gay. Not once. Not once during those two days.

He whispers/coughs something to her.

Humiliating. I'm going to a hotel.

Off.

DIONYSOS *closes the flat door, coughing all the while. The stage is empty. From the flat the sound of a guitar being played.*

GOD'S FIGHTER *drives into the hall on a motorbike. A threatening figure, he's wearing grey leathers, a dark helmet, a canister on his back, a large pipe wrench in his belt. He dismounts, the radio in his helmet is making a noise.*

GOD'S FIGHTER (*turns off the loudspeaker in his helmet, knocks on the flat door.* DIONYSOS *opens with a book in hand*). What are you reading?

He takes the book.

Fingering?

Suddenly shoves him to the floor, puts his knees on his arms, presses a thumb into the wrench. DIONYSOS *tries to scream.*

I know how you feel. I had something wrong with my voice once.

Cuts off a thumb.

Speech defect. Could only articulate vowels. The man with the cleft palate. Till I became a Fighter. I became one of God's fighters and was cured.

Cuts off the other thumb.

The dirtiest thing about people is their hands.

He stands up, places the thumbs in the canister.

Dismembered Dionysos. Time is nigh. The end is near. Good is already fighting evil. Evil is falling from the heavens onto earth. God is good. We must gather ourselves, those who love, those with a pure heart, so that God is victorious. Look at me. I believe. I am one of God's fighters. Carry his arms. The panzer, the helmet, the boots – and the sword of God – for the final battle.

Puts the canister back on his back.

Scream, if you can. Apart from you, the building is empty. No-one will hear you. No-one will see you. No-one is going to help.

Drives off on the motorbike. DIONYSOS *props himself up, looks at his hands. Loses consciousness. After a pause* ISA *comes onto the stairwell.*

ISA. Dionysos.

Pulls something out of her coat pocket. Tonelessly.

Your plectrum . . .

4 Spring

The same setting, only renovated. Music is coming from the courtyard. DIONYSOS *is sitting on the bench in front of the open window. He's wearing a white linen suit, has short, bleached hair, his hands are in his pockets.* LISA, *his mother, is a woman of around 50 wearing black, with grey smooth hair. She's holding a Havana.*

LISA. Such luxurious apartments. Previous tenants removed.

DIONYSOS. Michel and Mania are about to move onto the second floor.

LISA. You've changed.

DIONYSOS. My soul is blonde, mummy. The black comes from you.

LISA. Who says so?

DIONYSOS. She does.

LISA. Isa – and where did you meet her?

DIONYSOS. We fell in a builder's trench together.

LISA. Go on.

DIONYSOS. The world flipped over. Heaven fell to earth.

LISA. You're talented. Keep going. A writer must write.

DIONYSOS. I'm not a writer.

LISA. Write.

DIONYSOS. I'm a typical representative of the lost generation. Nothing that I do has any future.

LISA. Are there any glasses?

DIONYSOS. Not yet.

LISA. An ashtray, perhaps?

DIONYSOS. Apart from you, no-one smokes any more.

LISA. And how's the guitar going?

DIONYSOS. Progressing.

LISA. Sorry, I forgot.

He pulls his hands out of his pockets. They are mutilated.

Your thumbs. Like in the fairytale.

DIONYSOS. The dirtiest thing about people is their hands, he said.

LISA. Even when you had them you couldn't get a grip on anything. Any idea who did it?

DIONYSOS. One of God's fighters. I blacked out. She found me. I woke up a new man.

LISA. Isa . . .

DIONYSOS. You'll get used to her name.

LISA. And what does the father do?

DIONYSOS. Invests.

LISA. And where does the money come from?

DIONYSOS. She says he's just naturally rich. Ninety million.

LISA. And this is what I've worked for.

DIONYSOS. You and your politics.

LISA. You're making a big mistake.

DIONYSOS. Because I don't want to live my life like yours?

LISA. Marriage! It just turns the nightmare of a banal life into a dream from which there is no waking, only death. Do you want to go through life, one cog spliced to another cog until you grind to a halt?

DIONYSOS. If we're going to do it, then it has to be straightaway, she said.

LISA. Makes a change, you doing something you've been asked to.

DIONYSOS. Why did you never marry?

LISA. Do you want to blame me forever? The men. The books.

DIONYSOS. No . . . only . . . nothing ever lasted, mummy. After the wedding we get everything, the apartment, the house.

LISA. The future is certain.

DIONYSOS. You do that so well, sitting in a corner making disparaging remarks. Do you have to drop your ash on the floor?

LISA *drops her ash on the floor.*

LISA. I do. Where's the father.

DIONYSOS. Coming.

LISA. Are you sure?

DIONYSOS. She's sure.

LISA. Your housewarming party is nearly over.

DIONYSOS. If she said so, then it's certain.

LISA. You're in her thrall.

DIONYSOS. I'm her slave.

LISA. Is it true, what you told me last winter? That you'd never slept with a woman?

DIONYSOS. I'd never been in love before.

LISA. At your age. You're nearly 30!

DIONYSOS. I know what you think of me.

LISA. What do you like about her?

DIONYSOS. She loves me.

LISA. And you?

> DIONYSOS *is silent.*

Is that it? Is it enough?

DIONYSOS. She touches me.

LISA. Tell me, your mother, straight, that you love her.

DIONYSOS. Find a way to find a way to find a way . . .

LISA. Byron. Certain of it. A line from Byron. He wrote it in Greece, shortly before dying of malaria.

DIONYSOS. Find a way to find a way to find a way. A song. Do you know it?

LISA. No.

DIONYSOS. It's better than Byron. Life can be simple.

LISA. Here she comes. Every time I see her I get a shock – you've both got the same hair.

> LISA *walks past* ISA *in silence and out into the courtyard.* ISA *is in a light linen dress, short hair, sits down next to* DIONYSOS *on the bench.*

ISA. Well, what does she think?

DIONYSOS (*rumples his hair*). My mother. Three words with her and I'm exhausted, as if I'd been talking for hours!

ISA (*patting his hair down*). Don't get so worked up.

DIONYSOS. Dionysos! Me, my name, we all remind her of her visit to Greece.

ISA. Greece, how did an East German get to Greece?

DIONYSOS. By using her connections. My mother wrote travelogues. Spain, Italy, Greece. I destroyed her life.

ISA. Why?

DIONYSOS. She was forbidden to travel. She'd said I was the child of Zeus.

ISA. You're fond of her?

DIONYSOS. She's my mother.

ISA (*looks out of the window sadly*). Love is what one needs from a mother. And from a father. The air's pretty bad out there. Your friends and mine are determined not to get on. Everyone's pissed off because Kettling didn't come. And nobody likes grilled sausages . . .

DIONYSOS. Isabella!

ISA. Isa –

DIONYSOS. I enjoy losing myself in others' stories, because I find it difficult to talk. Especially about myself. Even before I've noticed that it's my turn to speak, my opponent is off again. Usually talking about themselves. So I have the sorry job of listening for hours on end without opening my own mouth. On the one hand, I don't dare, and on the other, I don't have anything to say. Apart from a few home truths. I'm a simple man with simple needs . . .

ISA. Get to the point.

DIONYSOS. I love you.

ISA. That's to the point.

DIONYSOS. Take your clothes off.

ISA. What about your mother?

DIONYSOS. She thinks you're nice.

They both go off, up the stairs. LISA *comes back in through the door, her Havana in one hand and a bottle of wine in the other.*

LISA. Dionysos . . . ?

KETTLING *comes in wearing a golden turban, an elegant suit, a book under one arm, a puppy under the other one.*

KETTLING. Hello.

LISA. Good afternoon.

KETTLING (*looking out of the window*). The happy couple not there?

LISA. Upstairs, in the penthouse.

KETTLING. It's a loft conversion, not a penthouse.

KETTLING puts the puppy down and pulls another seven whelps out of his jacket pockets. LISA watches him.

LISA. Unbelievable.

KETTLING. Afghan hounds. They grow two centimetres a day. May I introduce you. Aquamarina. They are all called Aquamarina. Spring litter. Winter litters are always weak.

LISA. Do you have a light?

KETTLING. Of course. I don't smoke myself.

LISA. But you carry a lighter.

KETTLING. For my daughter. I used to carry everything around for her. The lovely thing is, they never really grow up.

LISA. I don't like dogs.

KETTLING. My little doggykins. My lovely little puppywuppies.

LISA. Are you the father of the hostess?

KETTLING. Sadly.

LISA. I'm the mother. Mother of the host.

KETTLING. That Goth is your son?

He looks at her black clothes.

Hardly surprising.

LISA. You mean the black? I've been in mourning since his birth. Because he made me a mother. I never saw the father again.

KETTLING. May one ask, why?

LISA. His father was Zeus.

KETTLING. Zeus – I see.

LISA. She's widdling, your dog.

KETTLING. Where?

LISA. There.

KETTLING wipes up the puddle with a tissue.

LISA (*reading the title of the book*). Hebron – Abraham's place of birth.

KETTLING. A present for my daughter. A small memento. So she knows what she's missed. The whole of the Middle East by car. By Porsche to be precise.

He does not know what to do with the tissues.

LISA. Porsche?

KETTLING. It's not true that Afghans are stupid.

LISA. Are the dogs serious?

KETTLING. On the contrary, they're very friendly.

LISA. I don't like dogs. Do you know who Abraham was?

KETTLING. Just another father.

Ties the dogs to the scaffolding.

LISA. Abraham was the first monotheist. His father, Abraham, was still a polytheist. Carved gods for every occasion. One god for rain, one for sunshine.

Blows another cloud of smoke.

One day however Abraham announced that his father was mad.

KETTLING (*smelling the smoke*). What is that?

LISA. Havana. Are you interested in my story?

KETTLING. Havana? I'm interested.

Sits down next to her.

LISA. Abraham said his father was mad and left the house, which burnt down behind him – is the smoke bothering you?

KETTLING (*waving the smoke away*). On the contrary. It's reminding me.

LISA. Of Cuba?

KETTLING. Of a beautiful woman who smoked Havana's and knew Fidel Castro . . .

LISA. Fidel Castro.

KETTLING. I could watch her for hours.

LISA. Your Kreuzfeld-Jakob-infected brain, Kettling, is missing the point.

KETTLING. Kettling? Yes, that's me.

LISA. What do you think they're doing now?

KETTLING. Abraham and Abraham?

LISA. Our children.

KETTLING. What any couple does when they disappear from the face of the earth.

LISA. What we did then. In your brother's vineyard.

KETTLING. Lisa . . .

LISA (*blowing out smoke*). Abraham went up the mountain. He stayed there night and day staring at nothing, at the heavens. He soon got lonely. No stone gods for company, no wooden gods. He began to hallucinate.

KETTLING. Me too. Constant déja-vu.

LISA. And finally, in his loneliness, Abraham began to believe in a new god. An invisible god. And if we cut the story short, this god is love.

KETTLING. The woman you remind me of, I loved her.

LISA. So what is the story saying?

KETTLING. Lisa . . . Persephone . . .

LISA. What is the story saying?

KETTLING. Zeus and Persephone, two godheads making love in my brother's vineyard.

LISA. Love does not exist.

KETTLING. Why did you disappear? Behind your wall, in your east. I've been allergic to red ever since.

LISA. My little Trotzkyist. Now you look like King Croesos.

She gives him his book back.

Do you still believe in love, Kettling?

KETTLING. In love without specific object, yes.

He looks to the dogs.

I'm making progress. The result of my last visit to Moosbach – Aquamarina. I love them all, no-one in particular.

LISA. That turban, is it serious?

KETTLING. No, Lagerfeld.

LISA. What indomitable hair. Really thick, really impossible. It used to be crow-black. Boisterous hair that stood straight up. No question – it was dominant.

KETTLING. Dominant, yes. You didn't like that. What does your husband do?

LISA. Husband?

KETTLING. The father of your son?

LISA. He's still alive.

KETTLING. I'm a widower.

LISA (*frees herself*). There's something else, Kettling. My Dionysos, who is at present making love to your daughter, is our son.

KETTLING. Yes, yes, yes! Another point. How many's that?

LISA. You nearly missed it.

KETTLING. Our son . . . ?

LISA. Loves your daughter.

KETTLING. Don't turn our reunion into a farce, Elisabeth!

LISA. Life is a farce, Kettling.

ISA *and* DIONYSOS *come down the steps together.*

ISA. Puppies, how sweet.

KETTLING (*to* DIONYSOS). Well, my son.

ISA. May I introduce Lisa.

LISA. Not necessary. We've already met.

KETTLING. Hardly.

LISA. I have always hated families. I'm a writer. On the other hand, I do like clear relationships. What to do? That question's been around since Lenin.

KETTLING. There are always two options, according to Moosbach and the mother.

LISA (*after a pause*). Dionysos – your father.

KETTLING (*walks down the steps and takes the dogs' leads*). Who is this woman, this cloud of smoke?

DIONYSOS. My mother, she's a drinker.

ISA. Where does he know Lisa from?

DIONYSOS. I'm taking you home, mother.

KETTLING. What does she want? What does hair prove?

LISA. No Greek, no god. An investor.

KETTLING. I'm a shimmering person. Laughable perhaps. But I've a good heart, as Moosbach can testify. I'm predestined for compassion. Clear relationships. That was cruel. You know, your East was about the ugliest thing I've ever seen. Ugly and cruel. Between the Oder and the Elbe, someone had taken away all the colour.

Goes off with the dogs.

LISA (*to* DIONYSOS). Luck doesn't fall into your lap like a star from the heavens. Nothing is simple. Brother sister. One more story, a fairy story. Life is a farce. A malicious intermezzo.

V Summer Evening

ISA. What if we'd known beforehand?

DIONYSOS. As a sister you would have remained a stranger.

ISA. Sister, what's it like doing it with your sister?

DIONYSOS. I've got nothing to compare it with. I presume it's roughly the same as any man and any woman. What's it like with a brother?

ISA. Once was not enough to judge.

DIONYSOS. We'll keep the child. It's a love child. As your father once said: he'd be delighted if there were children.

ISA. He'd do anything to prevent it. As would your mother.

DIONYSOS. Father unknown. No-one can change that. Apart from the mother. And that's you.

ISA. You think we could live as a normal family?

DIONYSOS. You, the child and your brother.

ISA (*after a pause*). We'll keep the child.

Leans backwards.

A somewhat sombre moon and a lily-white Venus. The world is wonderful. Amazingly beautiful – great.

She shoots into the air.

DIONYSOS. We can always kill it later.

A thick carpet of clouds covers the clear night sky.